Protecting and Preserving
Your Family Wealth

Joe Goodman

LEGACY PUBLICATIONS

Rich Widows Live Forever

Protecting and Preserving Your Family Wealth

by Joe Goodman

Published by LEGACY PUBLICATIONS

Edited and designed by Armour&Armour, Nashville

Illustrations by Bill Ross

ISBN 0-9753337-0-4

Library of Congress Catalog Card Number: applied for

Order copies of *Rich Widows Live Forever* at www.richwidows.net. Legacy Publishing books are available at special discounts for bulk orders or signature editions.

For details, contact the publisher at P.O. Box 190522, Nashville TN 37219, call 615/627-4051, or fax 615/780-4497.

Contact author Joe Goodman at

Legacy Consulting Group, 213 Ward Circle, Brentwood TN 37027, 615/371-1011.

Second Printing

To my friends in the
Family Firm Institute

Contents

Introduction

People don't understand wealth.

Wealth is relative: A hundred thousand dollars may be pocket change to some, but a fortune to others.

And many rich people don't understand how to deal with their wealth. Most advisors don't understand what to tell their wealthy clients. And non-wealthy people don't understand what all the fuss is about.

Welcome to Wealth 101.

When most people think about wealth, they picture money and jewels, estates and yachts and vacation homes. Trust funds and dividends and inheritance. They all miss the point. By the time you finish this book, you'll understand that wealth is really about FAMILIES!

Building and sustaining family relationships is the essence of protecting and preserving your family's wealth. Whether you come from old money or just hit the jackpot, you'll only find happiness if you understand the family dynamic. In fact, money can buy a lot of unhappiness if you don't handle it right.

That's where this book comes in. You'll find two hundred axioms—some light-hearted and some hard-hitting—to stimulate your thinking about your wealth and illuminate the family system at its heart.

After each chapter you'll see lessons from the real world, where no one lives happily every after. Family advisors will especially appreciate chapter segments called "Professionally Speaking . . ." where I share techniques and principles developed by my consulting group for thoughtful financial and estate planning.

Don't try to read it at a single sitting. The book is purposefully designed for browsing. Not every topic will apply to your circumstances, but you'll see yourself (and your relatives) in many of them.

And don't underestimate these simple axioms. They comprise extremely important, even life-changing, advice. Many statements are direct and blunt, some even cynical, but all are designed to open your eyes and help you look beyond the technical side of wealth to the emotion-based issues and dynamics of the family.

We start with a look at the roles and relationships of family members: parents, spouses, children, seniors, in-laws, and step-families all have individual and interrelated problems. If you're a member of a family, you'll find yourself—and your personal issues—in these chapters.

Closely related are the issues of the family business: successorship, control, and ownership. You'll learn the politics of the family council and the value of the family office.

Relationships in wealthy families are governed by law: from marriage and prenups to divorce and alimony to death and estates. Technical agreements determine how family assets flow from generation to generation. Finding the right advisor, who can help you balance the technical side with the emotional, can make all the difference. You neglect the human side of these arrangements at your peril; it's all too easy to enable wealth to destroy your family.

Your wealth allows you to create a legacy that may finally give meaning to your life. With wealth come responsibility and accountability. Your stewardship of your family wealth—and how you teach your children to share their good fortune—creates a heritage of family values that makes you rich indeed.

1

Mothers,
Fathers,
Parents,
Spouses

Men and women, fathers and mothers, parents and spouses—all have different roles in the family and different ideas about the use of wealth.

Balancing the beliefs and needs of each member of the family may be difficult, but ignoring the problems can be devastating to the family fortune.

Let's start with a look at the relationships and interdependence between family members.

1. Mom is the most powerful member of the family.

The wife and mother naturally has the keenest perception of the needs and desires, the hopes and dreams, of all her family members. Typically, men are preoccupied by work, business, and financial matters (or golf). It is simply not considered "manly" to worry about emotional issues and dysfunction within the family.

But this is Mom's job. Although she can be reticent in a planning meeting—reluctant to annoy her husband by taking up the estate planner's time discussing "family things"—it is essential that her knowledge and experience be integrated into the family's financial and estate plans.

2. *The wife is CEO—Chief Emotional Officer—of the family.*

3. Financial planning for the family is pointless until absolute financial security is assured for Mom.

In estate planning for a typical couple, families have to face the fact that the husband probably will die first. In the United States, women on average live nearly seven years longer than men. The wife may be uncomfortable discussing this circumstance, but it is appropriate—and not selfish—to make her financial security after her husband's death the top priority.

Unfortunately, many wives also are uncomfortable communicating their strong need to be secure. Thus they need to be assured that ample financial assets will be available to provide them with a comfortable lifestyle and financial security for the rest of their lives. The estate needs to take care of Mom before gifts, transfers, or other financial distributions to the rest of the family.

Part of her problem is that Mom doesn't want to be the one depriving her children of financial well-being because she will live for a long time. Extremely wealthy families, of course, can more easily balance these competing objectives. It is much more difficult, however, to allocate limited financial resources for the surviving spouse and the children. In some cases, the wife's perspective of "how much is enough" for her financial security can be unreasonable or unrealistic, unless the family has adequate discussion and conversation concerning the financial plan.

4. A father must "anoint" his son[1] as his final act of greatness.[2]

Remember the movie *The Great Santini?* The father and son fight great basketball battles in their driveway. And when the son is finally about to win for the first time, his father resorts to cheating to prevent a well-earned victory. Instead of accepting his son's accomplishments with joy, pride, and new respect for his son as a young man, the father is determined to exercise domination and control at all costs.

Fathers must raise each son during childhood and then wel-

---

[1] *The concept of "fathers anointing their sons" is attributed to Dr. Frank Pittman, an Atlanta psychiatrist who first presented it at a meeting of the Family Firm Institute in the early 1990s.*

[2] *The concept of "final act of greatness" is from a booklet entitled "The Final Act of Greatness" by Craig Aronoff and John Ward, Family Business Publishers, Atlanta, Ga., 1996.*

come him into manhood at the appropriate time. Fathers must thus anoint their sons in order to complete their task as parents and launch their sons into their own journeys in life. As we see in *The Great Santini*, winning is important in business and sports, but selfish and unfair competition between father and son has no place in the family.

5. A mother must let go of her daughter as her final act of greatness.

The wedding ceremony is a symbolic act: Two persons first declare their independence from their families and then surrender their mutual independence for a life together as one. This is a healthy and beautiful process as long as parents don't try to preserve their former family. Mothers particularly have difficulty letting go of daughters. Mothers sometimes see a part of themselves in a daughter, who often is also a best friend. A mother may have strong feelings about how her grandchildren should be raised.

6. A father must respect his daughter as an independent young adult.

Fathers and daughters have a different relationship, so the process of anointment differs too. Fathers cannot welcome a daughter into womanhood in the same manner that he might anoint a son. But he must recognize and respect his daughter as a young adult, capable of being responsible for her own life, independent and equal among men and women.

Fathers must allow daughters to grow up. A father's role in a daughter's life does not ever need to end, but his role as a guard-

6. A father must respect his daughter as an independent young adult.

ian angel for a vulnerable child must evolve into mutual respect for independence at the appropriate time.

7. Accept the responsibility to learn about raising wealthy children— do not try to make it up as you go.

Many people suddenly discover they are wealthy—it's a pleasant surprise rather than a fact they grew up with. This new experience can be enjoyed and shared with family members, especially children. Unfortunately, many wealthy parents do not recognize that their children require special training and information to prepare them for their future responsibilities.

Raising wealthy children requires technical and psychological expertise. If you don't have personal experience dealing with wealth issues, seek competent professional advice. Don't try to "wing it" by trial and error. If you find yourself saying "I wish we had . . ." you've discovered too late that you made a mistake.

Wealthy families and parents have suffered success and pain for generations; take advantage of their experiences. Read, listen, and learn before you undertake the responsibility of teaching your children.

8. Many rich fathers deny that family emotional issues need psychological tools. They try to deal with every issue in terms of power, money, or control.

As we've seen, men generally don't recognize the emotional content of family issues. They often find their comfort zone in the business world of lawyers, accountants, bankers, and business advisors. Problems and solutions are straightforward. They don't analyze issues in terms of feelings, relationships, dysfunction, or emotional factors that often require assistance from psychologists or similar advisors. Men prefer problems they can choke with their hands or beat with a stick.

9. Long-lived parents can leave poor children— and rich grandchildren.

It's not uncommon for the surviving parent to live past the age of ninety. If she (or he) retains or restricts almost all of family's financial assets until death, the children may well have reached retirement age before sharing in the wealth.

These heirs have raised their children within their means and are entering their golden years without any experience or opportunity to address the responsibilities associated with wealth. Will the children now blow their inheritance on luxurious living and speculative investments? Or will they finish out their modest lives and leave the wealth to their own children? Either way, the next generation is blessed with sudden wealth without context, training, or experience. No wonder we see families go from shirtsleeves to shirtsleeves in three generations.

10. Increased longevity can be a financial disaster for children of well-to-do parents.

Adult children naturally anticipate the financial benefits of inheritance. But they're in danger if they make assumptions about any transfer of that wealth before their surviving parent dies.

The dramatic increase in longevity in recent years has resulted in tragic miscalculation by many adult children, whose financial plans relied on receiving a windfall before they retired. These children commonly carry large mortgages on substantial homes, lease luxury automobiles, run up credit card debt, and neglect to accumulate retirement assets.

Their plans fall apart, however, when Mom or Dad lives into their nineties. And their final years most likely will require extraordinary expenditures for health care and assisted living—dramatically reducing family wealth.

You don't want to be a seventy-year-old child relying on gifts from your ninety-five-year-old mother to sustain your lifestyle; make your financial plans as if you have no expectations.

11. Be thoughtful when the kids ask, "Are we rich?"

Hiding the truth will only make the children bitter, because they will perceive that you do not trust them.

12. If being rich is good, why do rich parents keep it a secret from the kids—really?

Many parents believe it is important to hide wealth from their children as long as possible, to prevent development of unhealthy attitudes, ideas, and ex-

10. Increased longevity can be a financial disaster for children of well-to-do parents.

pectations. These parents prefer that the children grow up in a normal household, uninfluenced by their wealthy circumstances until they are old enough to accept responsibility for their circumstances—say, around age fifty or so!

You can't teach children about the rewards, responsibilities, and burdens associated with wealth unless you make an effort to communicate with them.

Discuss and develop a program appropriate for each child and their individual ability to understand the importance of the topic. Do not assume it is better to wait until as late as possible to share this information.

---

13. Rich kids resent not being trusted with family wealth secrets.

---

14. Don't use wealth to control family members from the grave.

Trusts are wonderful blessings. Many of us can only imagine the freedom and feeling of luxury derived from receiving a trust-fund check each month.

Trusts can turn into problems, however, when a substantial bequest forces family members into long-term shared ownership of assets such as the old homeplace, the family farm, or the luxurious vacation house on the beach. Well-meaning parents and grandparents need to avoid the temptation to control their family from the grave.

No one can foresee the changes in circumstances that may

14. Don't use wealth to control family members from the grave.

take place ten to fifty years after their death. If you're creating a trust for tax or personal planning reasons, discuss its provisions with your lawyer and make certain you provide sufficient flexibility for substantial changes in the future.

What happens, for example, when valuable property is shared in a trust by a group of poor grandchildren and a group of rich grandchildren? Should family members who need the money have the opportunity to sell their share? What happens when some family members want to rent a property for income, whereas wealthier family members want to restrict the beach house for family use?

Consider whether income-only distributions that preserve the principal are appropriate when net trust income may average only two or three percent each year. Ask yourself why you should limit distributions if the beneficiary has a reasonable need or desire for the principal.

15. Rich parents should not try to use wealth to control, direct, or influence decisions that children need to make for themselves.

Think long and hard before stipulating that a trust beneficiary be a member of a certain church, live in a certain state, or live their life your way to receive trust income.

16. Each child is different—take care to customize your approach to teaching and raising each one.

17. The most joyful and satisfying hobby in later life is watching your children become young adults—serving as your successors and preserving your legacy—after you relinquish power, money, and control.

Family business owners often are guilty of postponing the need to pass leadership and control to the next generation. If children are not ready to assume ownership and management responsibilities by the time they're in their forties, will they ever be worthy or qualified in your eyes? Recall at what age you acquired ownership and control of the business. Was this a good or bad experience for you?

If the owner delays decision-making until very late in life—perhaps even until severe disability or death—the next generation's lack of ownership and management experience may be fatal to your legacy. If they don't have to sell it, family members may well run it into the ground because of inexperience.

Healthy transitions are essential. Transfer power, money, and control, well before your disability or death. Make yourself available as a consultant, as a peacemaker, as a wise source of advice, and as the most trusted advisor to your children. If you can fulfill this role, you won't have to ask, "What am I going to do if I retire now?" Enabling their success, and taking satisfaction in the healthy future of the family business, will give you plenty to do. Many couples look forward to their retirement years when they can travel together. But all too often, retirement arrives and one spouse is mentally or physically incapable of enjoying the golden years of travel and easy living.

18. Travel while both spouses are healthy—don't wait too late.

Not only is the impaired spouse depressed that he or she waited too long but also the other spouse is caught between retirement dreams and the responsibility of giving care. This scenario has plenty of opportunity for clinical depression and unhappiness.

Wealthy persons who have the flexibility of balancing work with pleasure especially will regret waiting until their sixties or seventies before enjoying retirement. Don't gamble with the possibility of lost opportunities.

19. Your wife tells you how wonderful and right you are, regardless of the objective truth—that's why you married her in the first place.

Your wife loves you and adores you unconditionally. She sees you only through rose-colored glasses. She thinks you are bright, hardworking, and an excellent family leader, as well as a good provider and loving father.

Shortcomings and disagreements are private: she can criticize you but will attack any other person who might find fault. Part of her duty is to support you and honor you. She desperately wants you to succeed in business. Your success will provide financial benefits and financial security for her and the children.

Your wife cannot be objective. Only rarely could she ever suggest that another family member might be a better choice to lead the family business. Only rarely could she ever explain that you receive an excellent salary for the work you do, and you should not rock the boat by demanding a raise from Dad.

The kitchen and bedroom are not the places to turn to for helpful, objective, and honest advice.

Husbands and wives: Please try to look past these stereotypes and recognize a sincere and helpful caution for loving couples who seek only to do their very best for one another and the family.

THE REAL WORLD

Background: Bob and Mary are about sixty-five years old. They have three children ranging in age from twenty-eight to thirty-five. Everyone enjoys good health. Two of the children seem happily married, and Bob and Mary already have two grandchildren with many more expected and hoped for.

Bob started a computer software business twenty years ago, ran it for only five or six years, and then sold it for approximately eight million dollars. He has done light consulting work since then. His wife quit her job as a certified public accountant shortly after the second child was born.

Bob and Mary have talked about financial and estate planning, but it always seems to get delayed before serious action is taken. They live a very modest lifestyle, and very few people are aware of their independent wealth. Even the children don't know.

Bob and Mary came to me for simple, standard wills—leave everything to the surviving spouse, outright or in trust, and then divide everything equally among the children at the death of the second spouse. They established trusts for family members under the age of forty.

Bob was upset when I refused to prepare new wills without exploring more details, even when I explained that their substantial assets afforded them significant opportunities. Bob said they could not work with me if I insisted on increased time and cost. (The wills would cost around three thousand dollars; I estimated a range of six to eight thousand dollars for more comprehensive services.)

During my initial two-hour meeting with Bob and Mary, I discovered:

● Mary is capable of understanding the technical aspects of financial planning, wills, and trusts if someone explains it to her.

● Bob selfishly did not want his wife to understand or appreciate planning options.

● Mom was closer to the children and grandchildren than her husband. She wanted to discuss ways to provide at least limited financial benefits to the children now rather than upon their deaths.

● Bob was more cut-and-dried and no-nonsense in his approach to financial matters.

● Mary had questions about the process if Bob died first and about the role of the executor and trustees of family trusts.

● Bob was obviously annoyed and emphasized that he did not want to "pay extra" for these discussions.

Epilogue: Bob was both proud of and secretive about his new wealth. It was his. He loved his family, but he was threatened by plans to share assets with them now rather than later. He thought the kids needed to learn to make it on their own without expecting or getting help from him.

The root of the conflict between Bob and Mary was obvious. Mary considered their wealth to be a family asset to be shared and enjoyed by all. To be sure, financial security for her and Bob was top priority, but she wanted to find a way to have financial security and share with the children and grandchildren sooner rather than later. She wanted enough explanation to make informed decisions about important planning matters. Bob did not.

I think Bob secretly planned to live to ninety-five and fully expected the benefits of wealth to skip his children, since they would be nearly seventy years old at his death. He feared the planning process would expose his vulnerability and shortcomings, revealing him as a selfish and greedy father, with a lack of "normal" concern for his children and grandchildren.

Predictably, Bob called the next day to tell me that they would use another attorney to "just draft a set of good wills for them."

Professionally Speaking . . .

The advice for professionals at the end of each chapter is drawn from the experiences of Legacy Consulting Group, multidisciplinary family business consultants and wealth advisors.

At the beginning of an engagement, our consulting group will work with family members to separate business and investment assets—the wealth—from the focus of discussion.

Family members are eager to discuss assets, financial planning, tax planning, and financial security, but these matters can be analyzed only in the context of the family system.

They're counting on you as the professional to lead them in the right direction.

First, concentrate on individual family members and their unique roles within the family group. Use separate interviews with individual family members to uncover secret issues or hidden agendas. Then, identify and explore family roles: the role of the mother, the role of the father, the role of both of them as parents, and the role of each of them as spouses.

Then and only then is it time to discuss the homes, the cars, the business, the investments, and the trust funds. Your solutions will be much more effective with this whole-family approach.

2

Sons and Daughters

In their parents' eyes, children are children whether they're six or sixty. This chapter's broad scope reflects the different issues and challenges that arise as children age.

Paradoxically, parental instincts put children at the top of the family's priorities yet prevent them from going their own way.

There are natural distinctions between the two genders and their roles in the family system. This is true even as we respect and celebrate the many similarities and equal opportunities afforded to men and women in the business world, if not the family group.

20. Rich kids need to sign their own income tax returns before age twenty-five.

Some parents insist on forging their children's names to their income tax returns. Though they say it's more convenient or saves time, in most cases these parents are trying to hide financial information from their children.

This might be understandable for younger children, but it becomes an issue of trust for older kids. Your good intentions can backfire, leaving your family in a situation like this: A twenty-four-year-old's trust fund from his grandparents was technically distributed to him at age twenty-one, but nobody told him. Now, his parents are scrambling to handle the situation because he just came home and announced his plan to marry his girlfriend. Trust and communication always solve more problems than they cause.

21. If rich children rarely interact with regular folks, how can they interact with the real world later in life?

Do not shield your children from the reality that they receive economic advantages and opportunities unavailable to almost everybody else. Sometimes, parents say they are just being protective, when in reality they are themselves uncomfortable facing the facts of economic inequality.

But if your children learn, worship, and socialize only with other rich kids, they're going to get the wrong idea that most people own a nice home, drive new cars, and vacation at the beach.

Only by experiencing how the rest of the world lives will your children understand and appreciate their privileged circumstances. Give your children plenty of opportunities to expand their horizons and interact with the rest of the world.

Whether your children are destined to be managers and professionals or only to collect their interest and dividends, they need to learn to respect the differences in education, economic opportunities, and circumstances that distinguish their families from others.

---

22. If your children attend elite private schools, make opportunities for them to interact in the real world that includes non-rich people and persons of different ethnic and cultural backgrounds.

---

23. Observe how your children treat the maid, the landscaper, the delivery man, the plumber, the repairman, the school teacher, the secretary, the waitress, the store clerk, and the salesperson.

---

24. Rich families should not act embarrassed about disabled children.

25. Special children (disabled, chemically dependent, emotionally unstable) need compassion—and special trust provisions.

Unfortunately, wealthy parents and their lawyers sometimes fail to give time and attention to the human side of estate planning.

Because each child is different, "standard trust provisions" may not be equally appropriate for every child and his or her issue. The estate planning process should include ample time for exploring current or future problems that could be addressed with special provisions.

Remember, wills and revocable trusts can be changed at any time prior to death or mental incapacity.

If wealthy parents are determined to single out one child for extraordinary restrictions or provisions, they need to communicate their thinking to the family or explain it in the will or trust.

Do not unnecessarily anger or disappoint a child without careful consideration. Your death is not the time for a child to learn of your mistrust or delayed punishment for a prior deed or action.

26. Use trust funds to support children who work for other reasons than money.

Your children's dreams may not include a high-paying career. Some wealthy parents resist a child's desire to teach, preach, do social work, be an artist or an athlete. Children forced into an "A-list" career end up totally miserable in the process.

Consider funding a trust to supplement a child's low-paying but rewarding career. It is important to formalize and fund the trust; unfortunately, your promises of future support could end the minute you meet your future son-in-law. Your support could actually encourage your child to follow his dreams while maintaining the lifestyle he's accustomed to.

---

27. Don't push a round peg into a square hole. Help each child find his or her slot in life, even if it's not what you want.

---

28. Maybe Junior or Missy doesn't want to run the family business. Can he or she tell you this without hurting you?

You may be very eager for your child to succeed you in the family business, preparing him or her from an early age. Your hopes and dreams may guide your child toward a particular role in life.

Be honest, though: What if your children don't want to follow the path you have prepared? Could they tell you that they'd rather be a schoolteacher or a musician?

Ironically, talking about this may be the most difficult in close-knit families. It is difficult for a child to burst his loving parents' bubble. Some children also will be concerned they may be financially shortchanged if they upset the plan of successorship. Open communication between parents and children can often strengthen and support plans acceptable to all parties.

Be very careful not to lure your child down the path you choose by promising financial benefits.

29. It may not be best for the children, and future generations of the family, to share ownership of assets.

Many times parents dream that all their children and grandchildren will derive pleasure and benefit from shared ownership of a vacation home, farm, family business, trust or other assets. This just doesn't happen in the real world.

Each child is different, and their families can have goals different from your own. Shared ownership may be appropriate in some families, but you need long and thoughtful communication with the younger family members who will receive the burden, or the joy, of a shared legacy.

In my experience, sharing real estate is not a good long-term idea.

30. Wealthy parents can easily sabotage a child's marriage with a carrot and a stick—don't do it!

Some wealthy parents can't resist manipulating their children through substantial gifts or promises. This is a dangerous game, even if you have the best of intentions. And you're playing with live ammunition if you involve your child's spouse.

31. Children, ignore your parents at your peril— emotional balance is more important than your share of the inheritance.

Be careful. Be smart. Ask yourself how your actions would be perceived by a neutral party.

Share an active relationship with your parents while you can. Show them you respect and love them on a regular basis.

Otherwise, you run the risk of remorse, regret, and guilt when you inherit wealth upon their death. A healthy relationship now can avoid more complex psychological issues.

32. Rich fathers will struggle to balance financial benefits for two sets of children if they don't communicate with everybody.

Rich men in a second or third marriage have unique problems in balancing financial benefits between the current spouse, children of the current marriage, and children of a prior marriage. Don't create a trust for your current wife that terminates in favor of children from a prior marriage at her death. Such a conflict of

32. Rich fathers will struggle to balance financial benefits for two sets of children if they don't communicate with everybody.

interest can cause difficulties in the future, especially if the second wife is nearly the same age as the children of the prior marriage.

33. A rich mother in a second or third marriage situation rarely has the same degree of challenge and difficulties.

This is perhaps because of her strong maternal instinct for all children. She may believe her current husband will provide long-term financial security for both of them, or that she will outlive him and divide her assets only among the children, as she sees fit. She may assume that the fathers of the children will provide for their children at the appropriate time.

34. Have your estate sale now, and prevent World War III from breaking out at your death.

You can't divide your possessions without arguments and hurt feelings in the family after you're gone. If you made careful plans and left clear instructions, they're quickly forgotten or distorted in the emotion and grief of death. More likely, you gave inconsistent instructions, or changed your mind, or just forgot. Or you promised a special item to two children to avoid disappointing either of them.

Consider a family disbursal event to transfer the art, furniture, household items, and other property before you're too old or too sick. It's much better to share beautiful memories with the recipients than create bad memories after your death. Be careful with jewelry and family memorabilia, which can easily ignite future warfare.

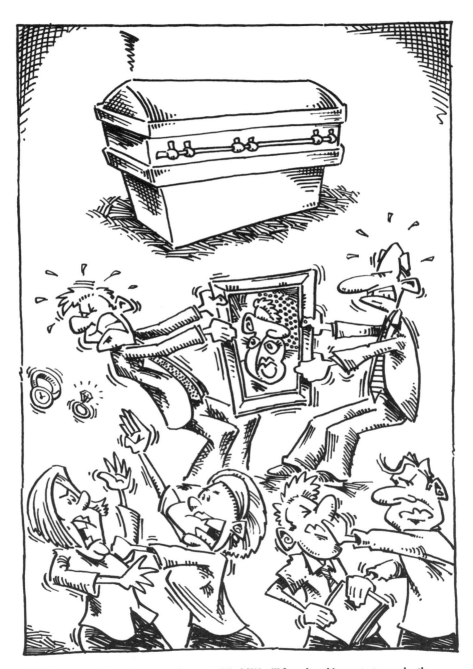

34. Have your estate sale now, and prevent World War III from breaking out at your death.

Otherwise, provide thoughtful and concise instructions to appropriate family members. Bereaved family members frequently observe "there would have been no arguments if only Mom had made it clear who should receive what."

35. Be suspicious if your child does not believe in prenuptial agreements.

36. Be suspicious if your kid insists that it is cheaper to own his or her first home rather than rent.

37. Be suspicious if your kid wants to join the family business straight out of school.

Business owners who value experienced employees mistakenly make exceptions for their family members. They often rationalize that "their mother wants them close" or "I want to be sure they're trained right." Or give their son-in-law a job to move his family back home.

Instead, encourage them to work for a while in a different company or career. If a child cannot work for anyone else, how can he or she can work under the supervision of you or someone else in the company? And children who jump to join the family business may need to gain self-esteem and self-confidence by proving themselves in another job. Outside experience will help them gain the respect of their co-workers.

38. Work to transfer family values along with family wealth.

Accumulating wealth to be transferred to the next generation is not enough. The preservation of wealth for future generations is most successful if family members who share current control, power, and responsibility have good values, morals, and objectives in their life. And they must transfer these characteristics to the next generation. Warnings, bribes, and threats will not prepare the next generation for carrying out the responsibilities associated with wealth. Family values handed down to all generations of the family will dictate the role that wealth will play in the next generation and beyond.

39. It is impossible to treat all children equally, so stop trying.

Unless you divide each asset into identical portions among the children, then it is not possible to treat the children "equally." Parents need to abandon this noble-sounding goal. No two children are the same. Also, their needs and desires will be strongly influenced by their individual families.

This quest for equality is often based on the unspoken fear that a child will be disproportionately advantaged or slighted — and thus angry and disappointed during the parents' lifetime and after they're dead.

Healthy communication with the children can help alleviate the fear and aid the best allocation of assets as gifts and inheritances for them and other family members.

40. Is equal really fair?

Should the distribution of wealth through lifetime gifts and inheritances focus on equality among children or on fairness? Equality and fairness are not the same, and equality may not always be fair.

It's appropriate to take into account careers, lifestyle choices, and the number of grandchildren in each child's household. You can consider dramatic differences in morals, values, financial responsibility, or other factors in making these important decisions. You may want to provide more for children in less-favorable economic circumstances than their siblings.

Don't feel guilty if you treat your forty-year-old child differently for stubbornly and persistently pursuing a "wasteful life."

Be careful. A lack of communication and understanding among all children with respect to these decisions can lead to anger and bitterness.

And one solution doesn't fit every situation. An outright distribution might be appropriate for one child, while another child may need a trust for one reason or another.

41. Many wealthy families allow one dysfunctional child to stymie the planning process for the entire family.

42. You are truly wealthy when you are concerned about leaving too much to the kids.

A good test to help you determine if you are truly wealthy is whether you consider the impact of wealth on your children. Many parents recognize that it is possible to give their kids "too much" or give it "too soon."

Discuss your concerns with relationship advisors and socio-psychological professionals, as well as such technical-based advisors as lawyers and accountants.

The impact of wealth is a legitimate issue that deserves research, analysis, thought, and communication. You need professional advice to identify reasonable alternatives and evaluate the attendant pros and cons.

43. Any of your children can run a valuable, low-debt business (into the ground).

A parent's reluctance to transfer management of a business to the next generation may be well-founded in some cases. Senior family members may harbor quiet and hidden apprehension, reluctant to hand over power, money, and control. Perhaps they secretly "know" that the successor is not qualified to assume the responsibilities of leadership.

41. Many wealthy families allow one dysfunctional child to stymie the planning process for the entire family.

Succession problems are only compounded when the business is essential to the financial security of the senior generation. The process is often postponed or sabotaged based on lack of confidence.

Unfortunately, it may take years to find out their suspicions were correct. A business with significant net worth, and relatively little indebtedness, can disguise the successor's shortcomings until it is too late. The company often deteriorates to match the successor's capabilities. By that time, the older generation is too old or helpless to undo the damage.

One solution for safeguarding succession starts with the company obtaining a bank loan and distributing the proceeds to the older generation. The successor now must function in a more typical business environment, with the bank keeping a close eye on business operations.

44. If Junior or Missy can't run your big business, cut the business down to size in an orderly manner.

This solution to succession issues may first appear to be a radical course of action. Conventional wisdom says a business must grow to survive.

But a business must also survive to survive. It may be financially prudent to extract equity from the family business and, at the same time, leave the successor with a smaller business that he or she can handle. Dividing one business into two or more separate entities can add flexibility to the strategic planning process.

45. Sometimes, a child and his or her spouse need to start their own family legacy.

If your children don't want to be your successor in the business, or lack the abilities and talents, help them establish careers suited to their strengths, talents, and interests. Bless the decision to create a new legacy.

46. Real issues must be addressed when a rich kid marries a not-rich kid.

Families have difficulty dealing with "mixed marriages" between rich and non-rich partners. Rumors, gossip, and innuendo often run rampant, and relatives do their talking behind the couple's backs.

This delicate and sensitive situation raises real issues that should be addressed. A not-rich husband often has trouble adjusting to his new wife's wealth. A non-rich wife may feel awkward spending "his family's money"—especially on herself. It's hard for either spouse to step into the life to which the other has always been accustomed. The advisability of a prenuptial agreement can be extremely difficult to address, especially if the topic is first raised late in the relationship.

47. No, Junior or Missy can't run the business like you have always done—but neither can you.

If your management does not change along with changes in the industry and the marketplace, then you will likely fall prey to the competition. Remember, a low-debt business

46. Real issues must be addressed when a rich kid marries a not-rich kid.

can continue for many years without change before it fails from bad leadership.

48. Recognize the natural strain in the relationship between the older and younger generation members.

It is not reasonable to expect old and young family members to have the same values and beliefs. Experience and environment shape everybody's viewpoints differently, and age creates differing outlooks. Senior family members, for instance, have a natural concern for financial security during their imminent retirement years. On the other hand, younger family members are enthusiastic about the time and opportunity to take risks, expand, and grow.

Tension develops from their different places in the life cycle. Older family members have capital, but declining energy; younger family members have energy, but limited capital.

Developing a balance between these competing interests require good communication skills. Learn to speak and listen.

49. Don't despair if children make isolated financial mistakes—you did.

50. Money can't buy perfect children.

51. Teaching children does not include controlling their lives or protecting them from the consequences of their bad decisions.

52. In measuring your children's ability to be responsible and accountable, take note of their listening skills.

53. Create a new legacy.

54. To the Next Generation: "Are you ready, today, to accept responsibility for assets and wealth?"

Youngsters often have a zest for exploration and learning. They may have a greater awareness of the need for successorship planning in the family business or for financial planning to appropriately share family wealth. Often, they are the catalysts in encouraging the family to investigate comprehensive financial and estate planning.

Although the focus seems to be on older family members, the impact of such planning has great importance to members of the "Next Generation." The decisions made impact their lives now and in the future. Before you gather the courage to discuss these delicate issues with your parents, you should take an objective look at whether you're ready to accept the responsibility for wealth.

Is your will up-to-date? Does it provide reasonably for your spouse and children? Do you provide financial security for your spouse not based on family gifts and inheritance? Do you have more than adequate property, casualty, and umbrella liability insurance to protect against the loss of financial assets to creditors? Have you given adequate attention to the appointment of executors, trustees, and conservators who would be responsible for the administration of family wealth and assets in the event of your death or incapacity?

55. Any kid with a Roman numeral after his name gets three extra bites at the apple.

All too often, the son carrying Dad's name receives preferred treatment over the other children. The son with the Roman numeral always has a good head start. And fathers often have a hard time recognizing that a son with a Roman numeral lacks the ability to succeed him as leader in the company. As adolescents, some "Romans" enjoy the challenge of seeing what they can get away with. Make sure you—and your Roman—recognize the responsibility and the rewards of carrying your name.

56. Primogeniture (favoring the oldest son) is alive and well in the USA.

In feudal Europe, the oldest son inherited the land, the second son entered military service (and probably died at a young age), the third son often became a clergyman, and heaven only knows what happened to any other sons. Daughters got dowries and made the best possible effort to "marry well."

Wealthy Americans demonstrate a great deal of gender bias, favoring the first-born son or sons in general. Some fathers still cannot conceive of a daughter succeeding him as leader in the family business. There is clear evidence of subconscious—or conscious—efforts to favor the oldest son (especially if he has a Roman numeral in his name).

57. In a new-wealth family, older children are often more appreciative of having money.

Older children are more likely to have experienced life without wealth. Their parents may have been building a new business or laying the foundation for investments that would one day become very valuable. The children remember a time of hard work, stress, and tight budgets.

Younger children often are spared the period of sacrifice, especially if there's a big age difference from their older siblings. This often happens when a parent has two sets of children.

These differing circumstances will have significant impact on their attitudes toward wealth. And they generate unique issues for the family, coloring perspectives and shaping relationships.

---

58. Don't pay a son a full-time salary from the business for a part-time effort.

---

59. Don't pay a daughter a salary from the business for staying home and raising your grandchildren.

THE REAL WORLD

Ted and Alice are in their early sixties, with four children ranging from twenty-five to forty-three. The two oldest are close in age, as are the two youngest. They have considerable wealth, but much of it is tied up in a family-owned business.

This family has fallen into many of the traps discussed in this chapter. The oldest son, with the Roman numeral III in his name, is trying to run the company without success.

Mom has always used money as a carrot and a stick to encourage the children to accept her opinion—even now that they are young adults.

The youngest boy married a small-town girl from a modest family, and it's just not the right fit, according to Mom.

Discussions of prenuptial agreements have caused problems more than once.

The parents still talk about mistakes made by the children many years ago.

The youngest child is predictably acting out after years of control by her parents.

Epilogue: The parents are good people; they mean well and want to do the right things for each of their children. But family relationships are strained because they failed to allow and encourage their children to develop individual lives. They tried to keep the family too close together. The relationship between the mother and the son who married the wrong girl has been severely damaged.

They sought professional help only after it was too late to avoid significant hurt, because they were embarrassed to think that their family has emotional problems. Even now, they are reluctant to listen to objective advice. And they don't want to spend money to get help for themselves.

Professionally Speaking . . .

You can't do proper financial and estate planning without carefully assessing and evaluating the needs and interests of the children. They should be active participants in the planning process, once they're in their twenties.

Be sure to make your evaluations early in the planning process. We conduct both formal and informal assessments to help collect pertinent information about the children from all family members.

Once the financial needs of the parents are assured, there are many exciting opportunities for the rest of the family wealth. You can't make any plans without considering the family dynamics highlighted in this chapter.

Related axioms from Chapter 1

4. A father must "anoint" his son as his final act of greatness.

5. A mother must let go of her child as her final act of greatness.

6. A father must respect his daughter as an independent young adult.

10. Increased longevity can be a financial disaster for children of well-to-do parents.

11. Be thoughtful when the kids ask, "Are we rich?"

12. If being rich is good, why do rich parents keep it a secret from the kids— really?

13. Rich kids resent not being trusted with family wealth secrets.

16. Each child is different—take care to customize your approach to teaching and raising each one.

17. The most joyful and satisfying hobby in later life is watching your children become young adults—serving as your successors and preserving your legacy—after you relinquish power, money, and control.

3

Rich Widows and Seniors

Senior family members are living much longer and playing an increasingly important role in the family. In many wealthy families, the most senior members occupy very powerful positions of control and decision-making over significant assets shared, either currently or in the future, among two or more generations. Our social system vigorously protects the rights and opportunities of senior citizens to maintain individual control over personal, financial, and business decision-making unless there is clear evidence of incapacity or disability. This situation is problematic in wealthy families with broad interrelationships and reasonable expectations about sharing and enjoying substantial financial assets now or in the future.

60. Rich widows live forever.

61. Rich widows live forever—especially stepmothers.

Trusts benefiting a surviving spouse can create many problems. All too often, they are created for tax benefits or "protecting assets" from a new spouse of the survivor. Or the trust transfers all the assets to the surviving spouse, providing more than enough for her needs and not enough for the rest of the family.

62. Rich parents live forever—they can buy good health.

Wealthy persons, especially women, enjoy a longer life expectancy than non-wealthy individuals. Better access to medical care, less stress about financial security, even not having to work as hard all contribute to longer life. As children, we celebrate the gift of long life for one or both of our parents.

63. Rich widow to friend: "I'd like to pull him out of the grave and shoot him." –Joy Culverhouse
The Tampa Tribune, 2/2/97

Typically, a husband can expect to die before his wife—this is simply an actuarial curse that men must live with. And the man is usually the spouse who wants to postpone long-term financial and estate planning for the family.

61. Rich widows live forever—especially stepmothers.

These two factors mean that wives need to speak up for their interests. After all, long-term planning is not for the husband's benefit, but rather for the surviving family.

64. How does it happen that a rich widow gets control of the family business at her husband's death? And does she really want it?

In a number of situations, wealthy wives have no opportunity to exercise control over family assets as long as the husband enjoys reasonable health. Upon his death or disability, the rich widow may naturally be concerned about someone else's assuming control of her assets and financial security.

But it may be a big mistake for her to assume she wants control of decision-making. This can be a huge responsibility, and many widows face the frustration of family members, friends, and advisors all competing for the opportunity to "help" her. Plan ahead for this possibility—or eventuality.

65. Rich grandparents are reluctant to make family gifts because they might need money to go to the nursing home.

Elderly family members, especially if they are widowed or divorced, can easily develop a distorted view of how much money they need for long-term financial security. And really, it's unfair to expect them to have a clear perspective on how much they need for living and health care under all future circumstances.

Usually, they decide that their current net worth is just the right amount. If they had a little less, it wouldn't be enough. If only they had a little more, they could make gifts to the rest of the family.

These unrealistic expectations prevent assets from flowing to the rest of the family when it could be most appreciated.

Using only an annual income to provide for living needs and health care costs is unrealistic and unnecessary. Annuitizing a significant principal sum can provide many financial advantages, including substantially greater cash flow than mere income can provide. These annuities can be purchased on a guaranteed lifetime basis.

When a grandparent lives on investment income and refuses to touch the principal, the assets are locked up until death instead of benefiting the children and grandchildren. Annuitizing the investments will generate greater cash flow until death. The estate pays fewer taxes. And other family members can receive assets over a period of years—with no reduction in the grandparent's annual income.

A qualified financial and investment advisor can offer advice on the many variations of annuities. More important, an objective advisor may be successful in reassuring the elderly family member that the plan provides enough money for living costs, maximum health care costs, plus catastrophic and long-term care. The advisor should be consulted before members of the family advance their own opinions and ideas, which will fall on Mom's deaf ears.

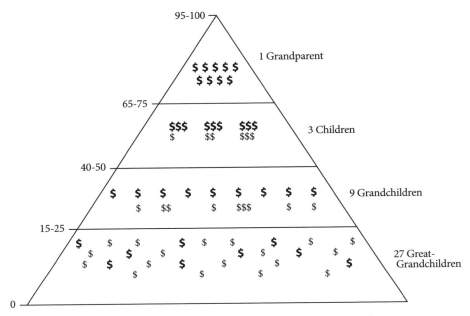

Figure A. From rich grandmother to grandchildren who range from poor to rich.

66. A rich grandparent doesn't mean rich descendants.

In this chart, only the elderly grandparent is truly rich. The three children experience some variation in wealth through their own accumulations and through marriage. The economic circumstances of the grandchildren range from very modest to very rich. The fact that all nine grandchildren descend from the same fabulously wealthy grandparent is almost financially irrelevant.

The perception remains, however, that they are all wealthy members of the same family; they equally share the same legacy, whatever it is. But economic circumstances are greatly diminished when efforts are not made to grow wealth.

67. Be very careful in screening and selecting care-givers for elderly family members.

Finding a caring, capable, and trustworthy caregiver for family members is extremely difficult, especially if you don't have experience. This emotionally charged situation only adds to the anxiety and concern you're already feeling about illness or disability.

Consider collaboration with experienced professional advisors who are familiar with specific alternatives and choices for your needs. Many not-for-profit agencies specialize in resources for health care and personal care-giving for seniors and disabled individuals.

Unfortunately, wealthy families need to exercise caution to prevent possible problems brought by an unethical or irresponsible caregiver. Sick or disabled family members are often vulnerable to the influences of their aides, especially requests for financial assistance. Even the most well-intentioned caregivers may succumb to the lure of the wealth around them.

68. If children don't share equal responsibility for caring for their parents, the family must have a clear understanding about financial expectations.

Sharing time, duties, and responsibility equally is almost always difficult. Some children are close by, while others live far away. Some are very busy, while others have more time. Some kids are just plain selfish. And each child has a different level of emotional attachment to and interdependence with the parents.

67. Be very careful in screening and selecting caregivers for elderly family members.

Because of this, the family needs clear communication about the distribution of financial benefits during the parents' life-time or after their death. One child may feel entitled to an equal share even after providing less support. Other children may insist that the principal caregiver accept extra financial benefits for their time, sacrifices, and services. Parents need to spell out their wishes and work out the family's differences before it's too late.

69. The grandparents' dilemma: Treat their children equally or treat their grand-children equally.

Parents have a strong desire to distribute financial benefits equally among their children. But what happens if one child has two children, and the other child has ten? The grandparents love all their grandchildren equally, but they've shared half the wealth with two grandchildren and the other half with ten.

The blessing of many grandchildren becomes problematic. They may prefer no distribution to hearing Billy ask, "Grandma, why don't you love me as much as my cousin, Tommy?"

In many cases, financial planners can work with the estate tax rules to equalize gifts among the family branches and among individual grandchildren.

Most importantly, adult children need to bless any reasonable plan of distribution for regular gifts, payment of education expenses, and other similar support. For goodness' sake, let your parents have some peace and happiness in sharing their wealth with grandchildren.

70. Rich people may have a better opportunity for longevity, but don't wait until your fifties to start healthy living.

71. Why is it a fourteen-year-old can't drive a car, get married, or control substantial assets, but his ninety-year-old grandparent can?

We protect our youth through limitations on decision-making but leave the elderly to fend for themselves. We have few legal safeguards to protect the aged from the effects of Alzheimer's, dementia, senility, undue influence, clinical depression, alcoholism, or other mental disability.

Often, the only recourse is to involve the court system and mental-health professionals in a formal determination of legal incompetence or incapacity. Typically, this depresses and humiliates both the elderly family member and the family. We must wonder whether the political and economic clout of senior citizens has taken the fundamental principles of freedom and liberty a bit too far.

How can a fifty-year-old child have a well-meaning conversation with a ninety-year-old father before he marries his nursing home sweetheart? The results are often wrath and disappointment, and, possibly, outright disinheritance in a moment of anger.

Families with clear channels of communication, strong love and trust, and a good sense of executing a long-term financial and estate plan at a reasonable time and age, will stand the best chance of avoiding disappointment or tragedy.

Unfortunately, even the best preparations can't prevent the consequences of near-incapacity or almost-incompetence, which can destroy wealth quickly.

72. Why won't the old man let go of control—really?

After many years of building a family-owned business or substantial investment portfolio (usually real estate), the family member in control is often reluctant to transfer responsibility to a successor.

First, the wealth has gained a life of its own; the senior family member sees it as another spouse or child. Second, the boss fears no one else can take care of his baby. And the problem is compounded because he cannot imagine filling the void in his life caused by transferring control.

Make successorship and contingency planning a part of the overall strategic plan to deal with the business or investment assets. And don't wait until too late. If the old man is sixty-five or seventy, it's time for damage control or other desperate actions.

73. Why won't the old man organize a board of directors for the family business—really?

One of the prerogatives of the family member controlling the family-owned business is the pleasure of "doing whatever I want to do without anyone stopping me."

This is a logical attitude for an enterprising entrepreneur

73. Why won't the old man organize a board of directors for the family business—really?

who would suffer greatly under close supervision or within an organizational bureaucracy. This is also true for family business leaders who simply enjoy the intangible benefits associated with power and control—deference, respect, awe, and praise (whether deserved or not).

But a business needs serious input from independent and objective members of a board of directors, formal or informal. If the family member in control cannot discuss issues and solutions with outside directors, the business has a major flaw in the governance system, which may greatly harm it in the future.

Don't be swayed by such excuses as "I can't afford to pay people to serve on my board" or "I don't know anyone qualified to appoint to my board."

74. The greatest loss of wealth occurs when the person controlling it fails to identify his or her own senility, dementia, or other mental impairment.

75. Business successorship planning cannot be discussed until parents' financial security is successfully resolved.

76. Older family members have a natural aversion to debt.

Many older family members have memories of debt and financial weakness, especially if they represent the first generation of family wealth.

Almost without exception, their road to wealth involved significant risk, including an unhealthy amount of debt. In addition, growing businesses typically have an appetite for additional working capital that must be provided by reinvestment of profits—and more debt.

Now they have the debt burden lifted from their shoulders. As seniors, they're ready to retire from the risk and competition of the marketplace and enjoy their golden years. But they remember helplessness and vulnerability caused by indebtedness, and it's natural for them to fear any situation that would bring back their former life.

They've earned the right to be free of debt; it's time for younger family members to deal with these issues.

THE REAL WORLD

I attended Mrs. Bradshaw's ninety-eighth birthday party at her posh condominium. Though her eyes are failing, her mind is alert. She has around-the-clock personal care assistants—only because she does not need any health care providers.

Estate planning years ago distributed substantial assets to children and grandchildren, outright and in trust. The plan seemed to provide more than enough wealth for her comfortable care and financial independence for her lifetime.

She possessed substantial wealth in earlier years, but much of this had dissipated through bad investments and unsound business ventures spearheaded by her children, all now around seventy years old.

Epilogue: The children are out of money. They had counted on receiving a comfortable inheritance at their mother's death long before now. They continually seek financial favors, gifts, and loans; the competition is fierce, and Mom would dearly love to accommodate them all.

Their hunger for wealth has made it necessary to appoint an attorney to protect her interests. In spite of what appeared to be prudent and conservative financial planning, her investment portfolio has suffered losses over the past five to seven years, and her funds are projected to run out in approximately three years.

It's decision time. The family must chose between taking chances with her mortality and leaving her at home or sending her to a nursing home for better medical assistance and much lower costs.

Professionally Speaking...

Approaching grandparents about distributing substantial assets to children and grandchildren is not easy. I use techniques developed by multidisciplinary professional advisors for discussing sensitive topics with aging clients. I try to emphasize respect for them, to assign top priority to maintaining financial security for the rest of their lives, to elicit proper expressions of gratitude from the children and grandchildren who benefit.

I stress the benefits of annuitizing financial assets sometime after age eighty rather than relying strictly on investment income for living needs. This assures grandparents their funds will not run out.

I also introduce the concept of *inter vivos* trusts, which protect assets from short-term or extended mental disability of the grandparent.

Older family members are more receptive to information and guidance from an independent, objective source, as opposed to well-meaning, but inartful, family members (or insensitive lawyers and other professional advisors).

Related axioms from Chapter 1

9. Long-lived parents can leave poor children—and rich grandchildren.

18. Travel while both spouses are healthy—don't wait too late.

Related axioms from Chapter 2

31. Children, ignore your parents at your peril—emotional balance is more important than your share of the inheritance.

48. Recognize the natural strain in the relationship between the older and younger generation members.

4

Prenuptial Agreements, Marriage, Divorce

The institution of marriage plays an integral role in society and in the dynamics of the family system, where it affects more than the bride and groom. The introduction of in-laws into the equation can have significant ramifications in the disposition of family wealth as well as in operation of the family business.

Nearly half of all marriages now end in divorce—an issue that's especially important when wealth is involved—but the power of love often obscures this reality. Somehow, intelligent young men and women suddenly become Prince Charming and Cinderella, focused only on "living happily ever after" when it comes to protecting the family's wealth.

A marriage contract plays a realistic, important, and positive role in the family financial planning process. Prenuptial agreements are increasingly accepted as a means of guarding against unintentional distribution or transfer of wealth outside the family "blood lines."

Such agreements seem inconsistent with traditional marriage commitments made by a bride and groom with stars in their eyes. But sometimes such marriage creates presumptions of ownership that may not always be fair or reasonable. Is it really fair for the surviving spouse of your son or daughter to inherit one-third to one-half of the family's wealth, as is possible in many states?

Because young people are increasingly wealthy as they enter their first marriage—and because second and third marriages involve serious financial realities—prenuptial agreements play an important and positive role in family financial planning.

Good communications and early planning can ease the emotional concerns and avoid ugly confrontations during an emotional and stressful time.

77. Do not seek marriage advice from a divorce lawyer.

Lawyers who devotes their career to divorce disputes often have a very cynical attitude toward marriage and divorce. Most spend their time helping couples separate and divide assets, not come together and merge assets. And they earn only modest fees encouraging couples to try to work it out, as opposed to large amounts for tearing marriages apart.

They're not a good source of marriage advice.

Consult a lawyer who specializes in wills and estate planning for couples. In his hands, a prenuptial agreement can be a tool to provide financial security and certainty in the event of either death or divorce.

The bottom line is that unless wealthy parents and grandparents have some assurances that their gifts will be protected from a divorce, they will be reluctant to bestow wealth on a married family member.

78. Rich daughters may marry the wrong guy.

Families have this attitude regardless of wealth, because parents are naturally eager for their daughter to marry a loving, protective, supportive man.

In wealthy families, however, this attitude can take on sinister connotations. The daughter's parents may not believe that her

78. Rich daughters usually marry the wrong guy.

new husband deserves to share in the family wealth or that he will make a good father for his wealthy children.

Parents, be careful what you think; you run the risk of alienating your daughter, regardless of your intentions.

79. Rich sons may marry the wrong girl.

Same advice.

80. When two rich kids marry, is it a marriage or a merger?

A wedding is a chance for friends of the happy couple to celebrate, and for friends of the couple's parents to congratulate. Are the guests mainly members of the upper crust of society and prominent business associates of the parents? Is the wedding an excuse for parents to rub elbows with power and money? If so, it's a merger, not a marriage.

A lavish wedding designed to impress people can put a sizeable dent in the financial statement of even wealthy parents.

---

81. Starting extramarital affairs is easy and cheap for wealthy persons. Ending them or explaining them is much harder and expensive.

---

82. Rich couples sometimes stay together for the money—two cannot live apart in the same luxury as together.

As wealthy couples age, sex and romance give way to new priorities. Arithmetic becomes more important: Living alone with a net worth of three million dollars is not nearly as attractive as living together with a net worth of five million dollars.

Why does a spouse put up with philandering? In some cases, a paramour can be accommodated for the sake of continuing long-term financial security.

83. Tread carefully around the prenuptial agreement.

The subject of a prenuptial agreement is inherently delicate, especially in a marriage between wealth and non-wealth. The non-wealthy spouse-to-be typically responds, "If you really loved me, you would not think a prenuptial agreement is necessary. Don't you trust me?" This may lead to discussion that the capacity for love and trust of both spouses is expected and demanded equally.

Sometimes love brings a naïveté that blinds even the smartest couples to reality. However unexpected or remote, the possibility of divorce—or death—deserves consideration.

Careful and respectful dialogue between the prospective bride and groom, and appropriate family members, should help to minimize stress and concern over these issues, especially if the communication process is facilitated by a trained and experienced advisor.

84. In some cases, a dying spouse may need to ask the survivor to protect their children by a prenuptial agreement with a future spouse.

Today's estate plan for the typical couple involves outright distribution of substantial financial benefits to the surviving spouse. Such sharing is an act of love, if not expectation, on the part of a married couple.

Sometimes, this attitude is tempered by a spoken or unspoken concern about remarriage of the surviving spouse.

The competing financial interests between the children and the future new spouse creates a tense and delicate situation. Suggestions from the children are usually not well-received when their parent contemplates remarriage. Perhaps the words of the dying spouse could have made a difference.

This awkward conversation should be facilitated by a skilled and caring consultant (rarely an attorney or "technical" advisor). who can help the couple discuss reasonable questions and concerns with love and understanding.

85. A postnuptial agreement can protect assets for the children, regardless of future actions by the survivor.

Wealthy individuals are probably familiar with prenuptial, or antenuptial, agreements executed between two parties prior to their marriage. Postnuptial agreements between spouses are unfamiliar territory.

These contracts (not valid in some states) are designed to clarify individual ownership interests of both spouses in their aggregate assets. In some cases, this may be no more than a division of jointly owned property, coupled with an agreement that a surviving spouse will not contest or elect against the will of the other spouse. Such an agreement can help allay the fear of a wealthy spouse that the survivor will be victimized by an enterprising new spouse.

86. Be suspicious of the fiancée who does not believe in prenuptial agreements.

Pre-marriage contracts are becoming much more acceptable as the divorce rate rises and burgeoning assets are brought into the marriage or acquired after marriage. Such agreements address legitimate property ownership rights and fairness.

Is it automatically fair that a survivor receive half of a deceased spouse's estate, even after a brief marriage? Should divorce be like winning the lottery of alimony and assets?

Objections usually come from preconceived notions and a lack of information about pre-marital contracts. People think pre-nups are cold and unromantic and indicate a lack of trust.

When the possibility of marriage arises, the couple should discuss the idea of prenuptial agreements in a healthy and candid manner. Each should receive advice from a competent lawyer. Remember, a divorce lawyer is not the best choice.

87. Be suspicious if the fiancée's father does not believe in prenuptial agreements.

I've noticed that the parents of a future bride or bridegroom are much more likely to be concerned—or offended—by a prenuptial agreement. Typical parents with modest means may consider their family assets as "ours together." They don't have the perspective of wealth that comes with significant assets. The father of the bride of a rich young man is the most common culprit, but he is not alone in the ability to do serious damage to family relationships.

Please get competent advice from an experienced advisor before starting trouble.

88. Rich parents are reluctant to transfer wealth to their children for fear much will be lost in a divorce.

Wealthy parents will often put off financial and estate planning. Though they cite time and cost as obstacles, in some cases the real reason is their concern about the strength and viability of a child's marriage.

Parents won't admit this, of course, but good estate planners need to explore the hidden agendas behind the failure to carry out the obvious need for financial and estate planning.

One child's unstable relationship should not hinder the planning process for the whole family. Such "negative planning" will only sabotage your effort to carry out a healthy and responsible financial plan.

Trusts and alternate gifts among family members can be used

to subtly, but effectively, address concerns about divorce, creditors, financial irresponsibility, and other factors unique to one of the children.

THE REAL WORLD

Robert and Sue inherited moderate wealth from both sides of the family. They had a substantial net worth as early as their forties because of proactive financial and estate planning by their parents and grandparents.

They have three married children. The daughter who married first did not enter into a prenuptial agreement with her fiancé. They divorced about two years later, and there were issues about his claim to assets given to him by her parents. (When she remarried, she requested a prenuptial agreement; it's rarely an issue the second time around.)

Robert and Sue insisted that the next daughter enter into a prenuptial agreement. Neither the daughter nor her spouse favored this plan, but they finally accepted a fairly straightforward and traditional agreement.

The young son was expected to do the same. But argument over a prenup almost destroyed the marriage before it commenced. The family attorney who assisted with the prenuptial agreement was asked not attend the wedding.

Epilogue: Robert and Sue are typical parents of an intelligent children with love in their eyes, significant assets already in their names, and more assets coming their way. They could not help but distrust the new in-laws.

Prenuptial contracts were very appropriate for this family. The children have have satisfactory agreements, and they have protected the family assets as far as reasonably possible. Larger gifts can be made.

It is now incumbent on the parents to end any mistrust about the future marriage relationship and any possible loss of assets in a divorce. They need to embrace the in-laws, love them, and honor each as a parent of their grandchildren.

Professionally Speaking …

We encourage wealthy families to allow us to meet with their young adult children as a group to discuss "the birds and the bees."

After we go over the pros and cons of a prenuptial agreement, highlight the positive features, and explain the seemingly negative features, we suggest that the children, as a group, adopt a pledge to other family members that they will enter into a prenuptial agreement with any future spouse. (See Appendix A.)

The pledge allows them to demonstrate to a prospective spouse that the prenuptial agreement is not a question of personal trust and love but a group decision made by the family to protect its assets.

Related axioms from Chapter 2

30. Wealthy parents can easily sabotage a child's marriage with a carrot and a stick—don't do it!

35. Be suspicious if your child does not believe in prenuptial agreements.

46. Real issues must be addressed when a rich kid marries a not-rich kid.

5

Trusts, Trustees, and Executors

You don't have to be the Rockefeller or Vanderbilt family to take advantage of trusts. Many families consider charitable, asset protection, business, real estate, and other trusts an integral part of an overall financial plan. These flexible planning tools address the special needs of individual family members—both young and old—when outright distribution of assets would be inappropriate or undesirable.

Trusts don't deserve their reputation as punitive or vindictive in nature (although some beneficiaries may disagree). Wealthy individuals have become accustomed to certain limitations on their abilities to enjoy financial benefits from the assets retained in trust.

You can't have a trust without a trustee. Family members must understand the duties, responsibilities, and power associated with the trustee and take steps to limit their control to prevent abuse or neglect of the office.

The role of executor parallels that of a trustee, but is limited to responsibilities immediately following the death of an individual in carrying out his or her testamentary plan.

89. The trustee is watching out for the beneficiaries, but who is watching the trustee?

Selecting a trustee for a surviving spouse, children, and other family members is difficult because a typical trust continues for a number of years. An individual who is an excellent trustee today may not be so capable in thirty years; banks and other corporate trustees may be inconsistent in hiring and retaining quality trust officers over the years.

Trustees have very powerful responsibilities. In most cases, the beneficiaries are either very young, very old, or lack the experience and expertise to represent their own interests. Consider an independent trust advisor—typically an attorney or accountant who knows the family—to provide oversight of the trustee. And be sure to provide for successorship of individual trustees, so a suitable replacement can continue to look out for your family's best interests.

90. Before you name your spouse as trustee, remember he or she may soon be under the spell of the new spouse.

91. Before you name your brother as trustee, remember he is busy with his own life and family needs.

92. Before you name your relative as trustee, remember he or she has always been jealous of your success.

93. Before you name your sister as trustee, remember she has always thought your kids are spoiled brats.

94. Before you name your brother or sister as trustee, remember they may be under the spell of their new trophy spouses.

95. Before you name your brother as trustee, remember he will be an eighty-five-year-old alcoholic on his third marriage some day.

I don't mean to pick on brothers. This statement applies equally to sisters, other family members, or any trusted advisor. Make special provisions for the forced retirement of a trustee if he or she is incapable of carrying out the duties of trusteeship; family members, trusted advisors, or the court can be tasked with the trustee's removal and the appointment of a successor.

Never make a family member a trustee without provisions for replacement.

96. "Bank and corporate trustee fees are outrageous." If you think this, ask yourself if you expect them to cut corners with your family wealth.

Very few individuals have the expertise and experience to determine the appropriateness of trustee fees. Expect to pay reasonable fees for trustee responsibilities, but demand quality performance. Choosing the bank with the cheapest fees can be a big mistake.

94. Before you name your brother or sister as trustee, remember they may be under the spell of their new trophy spouses.

97. "Bank and corporate trustee fees are outrageous." If you think this, ask yourself, "Compared with what?"

You should not expect a non-bank trustee to perform trust duties and for a substantially lower fee than a bank. It's possible to induce a trustee to serve for a minimal fee, but you'll get very little in terms of investment analysis and trust administration.

This is not in your family's best interests.

Remember, trustees' fees are typically deductible for income tax purposes, and the cost should be very low compared to the trust fund principal amount.

98. "The bank did a terrible job with my mother's trust." When you hear this, remember there are two sides to the story.

Beneficiaries are rarely qualified to judge the legal, fiduciary, and investment capabilities of a bank or corporate trustee. In many cases, substantial assets are held in trust for a good reason: because the beneficiary lacks the ability to deal with sophisticated financial and technical responsibilities.

99. "The stupid bank 'sits on' the trust my parents established for me, and I get almost nothing out of it." Remember, that's why the parents put wealth in trust in the first place.

Parents may have good reasons to limit a beneficiary's income. On the other hand, an income-only trust may not be the best choice, especially when dividend and interest rates are extremely low. When you're setting up a trust, consider giving the trustee discretion or direction to distribute portions of trust principal from time to time.

100. "Because of the stupid bank, my trust has not grown at all in twenty years."

This common complaint is heard most often from children who become trust beneficiaries after their surviving parent dies. In many cases, the family member creating the trust stipulated that the trustee invest assets for the primary purpose of producing current income. Asset growth and appreciation in value are secondary priorities.

Some trusts require that the funds must be invested in bonds, U.S. Treasury obligations, or other fixed-income investments, all of which have very little opportunity for growth and appreciation. Usually, these trusts are relatively small and may be inadequate in generating income through a more balanced investment philosophy.

Disappointed beneficiaries often are selfish or lack objectivity—the trust may be treating them the way they deserve.

101. Why do some wealthy parents prefer trusts for daughters, but not for sons—really?

Some fathers, in particular, still can't conceive of daughters handling money wisely and making smart financial decisions.

---

102. There is no such thing as a simple trust.

---

103. The promise of annual financial support can never take the place of a trust or annuity.

Some parents mistakenly make promises to children rather than take concrete action. They may think the loving family relationship precludes the need, or even desire, for a written contract.

But they may be using these promises as an incentive to force children into following their wishes. Consider a child pursuing a dream to be a schoolteacher instead of joining the family business as the parents expect. The parents may seem supportive, promising to provide financial support. But what happens if the child chooses to teach school on an Indian reservation rather than at the family's favorite private school?

Parents making promises retain too much power and control, and children need to be cautious in this situation. A promise is no substitute for creation of a trust fund or purchase of an annuity contract.

104. Trusts that pay only income for the life of a beneficiary may not be wise.

Many parents don't understand that a million-dollar trust fund may not produce more than thirty to forty thousand dollars in annual income, especially after taxes, trustee fees, and other expenses are paid. Trustees often invest a significant portion of assets in stocks and other securities with an extremely low rate of return. Income is also dramatically affected by prevailing interest rates.

Ask yourself why you are limiting the children to income when it is your long-term intention for them to enjoy the funds as they age.

Ask your estate planner and financial advisor about the alternatives. For example, you can provide that annual distributions shall be the greater of income or six percent of the fair market value of the trust principal determined annually. Trust beneficiaries can have limited power to withdraw up to five percent of the value of the trust each year, in addition to the distribution of annual income. Incentive trusts may pay additional amounts based upon the annual earnings of a beneficiary.

And don't try to make one trust cover the entire family. Different family members may need differing protection or support.

105. Before you name your brother as executor, consider axioms 91–95 above.

The responsibilities of an executor begin with the death of an individual and will end when the estate is closed by the probate court, usually a period of one to three years. Executors have extremely broad powers in dealing with the assets and liabilities of the deceased. Consider the need for checks and balances, such as appointing co-executors or a special advisor to prevent abuse of power.

106. Before you name your oldest child as executor, remember he or she never did get along with brothers and sisters growing up.

Parents often have a difficult time choosing among their children in the appointment of executor (or trustee). For wealthy families, the executor can have a dramatic impact on the value of significant assets—and on the distribution of assets among family members.

In many cases, favoritism may be subtle and subconscious. In other cases, a child may use his or her power as an opportunity to right past wrongs, perceived or real.

But avoid naming all children as co-executors, which greatly increases the costs and precludes prompt, decisive decision-making.

107. Before you name your oldest child as executor, remember he or she will be under the spell of his or her spouse.

108. Before you appoint family members as executor or trustee, carefully explore possible conflicts of interest.

Second marriages, stepparents and stepchildren, or children by more than one marriage are usually the source of conflicts of interest. Regardless of the apparent love and harmony surrounding you, your death leaves considerable room for problems and discord, especially if your family has avoided healthy communication over the years.

THE REAL WORLD

John leaves an apartment building in trust for life of his second wife Mary (not the mother of the children). He names two of his children as co-trustees because they are capable property managers and because the ex-son-in-law wants to avoid fees for outside management or corporate trusteeship. He expects the net rental income each year to be distributed to Mary (the trustees' stepmother) until her death, when the property would be distributed equally to his children.

Soon after his death the children sold the building and invested the funds in the stock market. The estate paid huge legal fees before the matter was settled.

* * *

Jim names his brother Tom as trustee for his children until they're forty years old. The trust includes Jim's share of a farm and family-owned business. The trust document contains standard broad language allowing Tom to make investment decisions, including typical expressions of absolute discretion, plus indemnity clauses, all of which are more commonplace for corporate and bank trustees.

Tom immediately developed numerous conflicts with his nieces and nephews over farm-related decisions, annual dividends from the family business, and compensation paid to himself as president of the company. The estate paid huge legal fees before the matter was settled.

* * *

Charles is a dentist who appointed his wife and oldest son as co-executors of his estate. After his death, the value of his practice began to erode quickly as patients found new dentists.

The son quickly found a buyer, but his mother held out for a higher price. She had been assured by Charles that the practice's value would provide her with substantial financial benefits.

The dental practice was sold nearly a year later for approximately one-quarter of the price the son had negotiated. The family is still not speaking to each other.

* * *

Bob visited several bank trust departments to negotiate lower trustees' fees, but he eventually decided that
even the lower fees were "too high." He appointed his
son (the one with Roman numerals after his name) as sole
trustee to manage substantial investment assets.

After Bob's death, the son made good-faith efforts to
invest the liquid funds with assistance from friends associated at reputable brokerage firms. The trust benefited his
seventy-year-old mother, with equal distribution among
the three children at her death.

The son's own brokerage account had increased dramatically in the 1990s through investments in such high-
tech investments as Lucent and WorldCom. Eager for his
mother and siblings to enjoy similar success, he invested a
considerable portion of the trust fund in high-tech stocks
just before they collapsed in 2000.

An arbitration hearing against one of the brokerage
firms predictably found in the firm's favor. Recovery from
the son's professional liability insurance carrier was like-
wise unsuccessful. After considerable discussion, the family decided not to sue the son.

Epilogue: The common lesson from these examples is
simple: The money you spend to get good advice and reli-
able expertise pays for itself many times over.

Professionally Speaking ...

Don't expect family members to choose trustees and executors unless they have adequate background, training, and information about alternatives. A quick answer may make a simpler job of preparing the will or trust document, but that's a disservice to the client.

We never ask clients to nominate a trustee or executor until they have completed a series of exercises, discussions, and role-playing designed to highlight the positive and negative attributes of each possible choice. Often, clients with a high degree of confidence in a specific trustee or executor may not be aware of the conflicts, issues, and problems that may develop years down the line.

We also make sure the client considers the need of a successor trustee or executor, an important point often overlooked in the planning process.

Related axiom from Chapter 1

14. Don't use wealth to control family members from the grave.

Related axioms from Chapter 2

25. Special children (disabled, chemically dependent, emotionally unstable) need compassion—and special trust provisions.

26. Use trust funds to support children who work for other reasons than money.

6

In-Laws and Stepfamilies

Marriage creates a natural extension of the family through the acquisition of in-laws. When wealth is involved, interactions with in-laws become more complex and delicate. Are they considered "part of the family" or not?

Remember, every married son and daughter also is an in-law in another family. Grandchildren share the heritage of two or more families. Half of all parents also were once in-laws, members of another family, before becoming a senior family member.

The traditional nuclear family—two parents in a fifty-year marriage with children together with marriages and grandchildren that replicate the process—is becoming increasingly rare. Divorce and remarriage is becoming more prevalent. Increased longevity means more remarriages after a spouse dies.

Although such terms as *stepmother, stepfather, stepson*, and *stepdaughter* have become familiar terms, Walt Disney's stereotype of the wicked stepmother has done a lot of damage in multifaceted families.

Fortunately, blended families are now more acceptable in our society, relieving tensions but making good communication and careful financial planning more and more essential.

109. Be suspicious if your daughter-in-law admires your jewelry, art, silver, china, and crystal.

Your son and his wife will understandably discuss future gifts and inheritances from you. The danger comes when your daughter-in-law becomes impatient enough to bring the issue into the present tense, instead of the future. This can open up a quiet competition among all children and in-laws.

110. Be suspicious if your son-in-law admires your car and vacation home.

It works both ways!

111. You are rich when you love your in-laws and they love you.

Many members of a family forget that they were once outsiders, sometimes viewed with caution and suspicion. After many years, the distinction between blood relatives and long-time spouses becomes blurred. (Notice how little distinction is made between an aunt and uncle, though one is a blood relative and one is not.)

At some point, in-laws need to be accepted as an integral part of the family. After all, your grandchildren possess just as much blood and genetic material from your son- or daughter-in-law as they do your son or daughter.

Rather than worry about the consequences of their possible divorce, join your children as they celebrate the prospect of a long and happy life with their chosen mate. Go ahead and take the plunge: Fall madly in love with your in-laws and accept them as your adopted children. After all, they have sworn an oath to "do right" by your son or daughter.

Holidays and vacations will be much more fun. And you will see more of your grandchildren.

112. Ignore your in-laws at your peril.

110. Be suspicious if your son-in-law admires your car and vacation home.

113. Woe be unto the daughter-in-law who takes sides in a family dispute.

Even the most violent fights between siblings are often followed by forgiveness and reconciliation. But family bystanders—especially in-laws—should be extremely careful before they take sides by offering support or criticism.

Long after the participants forgive and forget, memories of the criticism (even if it's merely a wife defending her husband) will raise resentment; families have a natural reaction to rally together against an "outsider."

114. If an in-law is the best person to lead the family business or family financial matters, don't let fear of future divorce prevent the right choice.

115. Two spouses in a second marriage create a disaster for the family of the first spouse to die by trying to share a simple estate plan.

The country's high divorce rate has increased the incidence of second (and third or fourth) marriages. Estate planning for such "dynamic couples" is inherently more complicated when there are children of prior marriages plus children of the current marriage.

Unfortunately, many couples in these circumstances ignore reality and rely on promises of future support. They expect that the surviving spouse will allocate assets among all the children as they have agreed. The distribution of financial benefits becomes a lottery based on which spouse outlives the other.

Blended families must undertake careful and caring analysis about sharing of financial benefits. Don't jeopardize the legacies of children from your first marriage because making plans makes you uncomfortable. Experienced estate planners can help facilitate non-threatening communication between all parties.

THE REAL WORLD

One very tight-knit family shares almost everything, going to church together, vacationing together, and owning a third-generation family business together.

This business employed two sons-in-law. After a very difficult divorce, everyone was certain the ex-son-in-law would be forced to leave the company, but ten years later, he's still working in his (ex-)family business at a supervisory level.

The other son-in-law is chief financial officer, and time after time his advice to the company holds more power than any (blood) family member.

Epilogue: This family is one of my favorites. Even I am caught off-guard by their ability to separate family issues from business matters under very difficult circumstances.

The family that embraces its in-laws, and can separate the business from the family, will be richly rewarded.

Professionally Speaking...

When undertaking comprehensive planning for multi-generation family groups, we know we must eventually challenge the family's culture and its philosophy toward in-laws.

Usually, families either want to keep their wealth confidential and at some distance from the in-laws, or they support open information and shared decision-making.

We try to point out that sons- or daughters-in-law also are the parents of the grandchildren. We remind family members who insist assets "remain in the bloodlines" that the blood of in-laws is generously mixed in their own. Sometimes, a parent who uses the excuse, "I'm only trying to protect the family assets that rightfully belong to lineal descendants" is actually trying to rationalize gamesmanship.

When appropriate, we also ask, "When did you stop being an in-law and become a blood member of the family?" (This is more applicable in terms of old money rather than new wealth.)

Related axioms from Chapter 2

32. Rich fathers will struggle to balance financial benefits for two sets of children if they don't communicate with everybody.

35. Be suspicious if your child does not believe in prenuptial agreements.

Related axiom from Chapter 4

87. Be suspicious if the fiancée's father does not believe in prenuptial agreements.

7

Ownership, Control, and Successorship, of the Family Business

Many wealthy families share ownership of a business, often the dominant asset in their portfolio. The family-owned business adds complexity and complication to the financial planning process.

Dynamics associated with the family system overlap with those of the business system. The boundaries are blurred in many situations, making it nearly impossible to discern whether the family system or the business system is the origin of particular problems and issues.

Professional facilitation is essential, and clear and open communications among family members takes on heightened importance. Business decisions may affect the welfare of family members not even active in the business.

You'll eventually transfer this wealth to future generations; the way you pass the torch will affect your family legacy in the community and beyond, for many generations.

116. Selling the family business may be the best option. Move your legacy to another memorial site.

A majority of family-owned businesses fail to survive to the second or third generation. Sometimes succession issues are the source of the problem. The family may lack a qualified successor but be unwilling to entrust leadership to a non-family member.

Typically, families do everything they can to continue a family-owned business for another generation, often as a family legacy or a memorial to ancestors. Selling the business is just not an option even if professionals advise them to.

You risk loss of substantial wealth by hoping that your chosen successor might someday grow into the job or become a worthy leader. Do not let your desire to establish—or maintain—a legacy override good judgment.

Painful as it may be to you and family members, selling the family business is sometimes the right move. Use the proceeds to create a new legacy for the family: a charitable foundation, a building or monument, or another business.

Family decision makers need to accept the responsibility to make this choice if it brings the most benefit to the family.

117. Pass the torch, but be sure to tell the recipient it's hot.

You have to let go when you pass the torch, and someone else has to grab it. You and your successor both have important responsibilities. You need to ensure continuity of the legacy by providing wisdom, assurance, and confidence. Recipients need to acknowledge the serious nature of their anointment with humility, awe, and gratitude. Being appointed to leadership carries automatic responsibility for the welfare and security of many other family members.

118. Passing the torch doesn't have to mean burning down the family tree.

You can choose to do it right, or you can choose to make a mistake. But be assured, you will have to pass the torch someday.

119. Successorship is a process, not an event.

Senior family members who possess power, money, and control like to think that relinquishing their leadership will be an event of their own time and choosing. Many times death makes the choice for them, leaving the business without a leader at a critical time.

Make it a priority now to create a strategic plan for successorship in your family-owned business; it takes three to five years in most cases.

117. Pass the torch, but be sure to tell the recipient it's hot.

120. Successorship will be decided in the limousines during your funeral procession if you don't do it beforehand.

Cell phones have greatly enhanced this activity.

121. You can't select a successor by flipping a coin on your deathbed.

If you don't make succession plans, your business will face chaos and tragedy when power must be transferred because you're dead. Being uncertain about the correct choice is not a good excuse. Being unable to choose between relatively equal alternatives is not a good excuse.

Make your decision and tell the family as soon as possible, or better yet, include the family in the decision-making process. You'll avoid causing anger and disappointment at such an emotional time as your death or disability. And your family will have the opportunity to adapt to their future roles in the family business or explore different careers with your help and support.

122. Are key non-family managers subconsciously sabotaging the process for family successorship?

Non-family managers naturally are threatened by a change in the leadership of your family business. To alleviate uncertainty and anxiety, let members of management actively participate in the strategic planning process for successorship. They may even get excited about new leadership and new opportunities—not to mention their joy at getting rid of the old goat.

123. It is better to accept the fact that issues are interrelated in a circle than to struggle down a spiral staircase.

Issues of the family, wealth, business, financial planning, estate planning, and investments share important interrelationships that are circular, not hierarchical. Any decision-making discussions must include consideration of the effects, direct or indirect, on all the other issues.

You can, however, inadvertently create a three-dimensional circle that evolves into a descending spiral. Without making extra effort, your communication and decision-making may move in a downward circular direction, becoming increasingly negative and frustrating.

Strive to keep the planning process in a single-plane circle—and be prepared to go around the circle more than once before answers and solutions reveal themselves.

---

124. The process of direct, honest, and regular communications within the family is the key to future successorship and legacy.

125. If neglected, abused, or taken for granted, a golden goose can slowly die from a broken heart.

Wealth rarely stands still, constantly moving either forward or backward. If your wealth is concentrated in only one or two assets, you face a substantial risk of loss over a period of time.

Your golden goose needs active care and attention, especially from those who have the power and control to make important decisions. Your trusted financial advisors cannot provide assistance if they don't know your long-term strategic plan—especially if you don't have one!

Activity and interest on the part of appropriate family members in carrying out responsibilities associated with wealth is best the way to avoid unnecessary risks and problems.

126. Conduct an emergency fire drill; what will happen if you die or become incapacitated today?

Sometimes, the only way to ensure that comprehensive estate and financial planning receive adequate attention is to yell "Fire!" Pretend that the key family member is suddenly incapacitated or dead and assess the situation in terms of the family, the family business, and the preservation of wealth.

This exercise is an eye-opening experience for family members (and their spouses) with significant responsibilities for family assets and wealth. And it's easier to relate to than having to read multiple accounts of families and kingdoms destroyed after their leader's death.

126. Conduct an emergency fire drill; what will happen if you die or become incapacitated today?

127. Consider making an audio record of your hopes, beliefs, wishes, thoughts, and suggestions for the family and the business after your death or incapacity.

128. The time, effort, and expense of strategic family business planning greatly increases the odds of success.

129. Be suspicious when a family member insists that he or she must have fifty-one percent of the voting power.

People can easily rationalize why they should control a family-owned business or other assets rather than sharing voting power. Think twice before installing a dictatorship (even a benevolent one) in the family group. Even if one child is extraordinarily talented, loyal, and capable, it is often a mistake to put one sibling in a position of power and control over other family members.

Still, appropriate power and control may need to rest in the next generation with disproportionate voting rights (e.g., three children get twenty-four percent each, and one gets twenty-eight percent). You may be better off accepting the possibility that two or more shareholders will gang up on one sibling and force a sale.

130. Do not use a family council to control family members.

Periodic meetings can encourage large, wealthy families to discuss matters of mutual interest, especially if the family shares broad ownership of a business or substantial investment assets.

The structure of a family council provides a quasi-formal organization for the whole family to meet, retreat, share decision-making, attain economies of scale with financial and investment products and services, and simply enjoy their legacy together.

But beware if the initial idea for a family council arises from the branch that has the most control over the family wealth. This power is often centralized with a small group of individuals, who could be seeking to maintain the status quo. Other family members may be trying to consolidate power among several minority interests.

These structures can be extremely beneficial, however; just be sure to get assistance from an objective and qualified advisor.

131. Don't assume that cousins will always vote along family branches.

Block voting is natural in families, especially when power is shared among three or more siblings. Voting control erodes, however, as power is transferred to succeeding generations. Eventually, the family business may be controlled by a loose consortium of cousins and will then assume the characteristics of a quasi-public corporation.

Senior family members should avoid being obsessed with preserving long-term control within a particular branch of the family. Many family business consultants advocate limiting ownership within branches to maintain control among family members active in the business. This makes sense in many cases, but is undesirable or impractical in many other situations.

132. Why do people with power, money, and control try to make decisions without knowing all the facts, alternatives, and lessons from others?

When people talk about the "changes" in a person with power, they're usually referring to development of strong leadership skills. An early period of awe and humility gives way to greater self-confidence as each success is followed by another. But strong leaders need to recognize the importance of acquiring information before making decisions. As the ruler grows older and the kingdom grows larger, he has increasingly difficulty grasping all the important facts, factors, and information without help.

133. The golden goose that produces bounty for only one master will be divided into many parts at the master's death.

The owner's prerogative is to enjoy the wealth or share it with other family members, especially if it's earned wealth or first-generation wealth.

You have no obligation to distribute financial assets to children, grandchildren, and other family members. In most states, a surviving spouse has the right to a portion of the estate, but children have no such right.

Healthy communication can help you avoid many potential problems with the family. The unilateral exercise of control over wealth, without discussion or explanation, forms fertile ground for breeding discontent and problems within the family system.

134. You can face your own mortality if you can voluntarily surrender power, money, and control to your successors.

You'll see your legacy reveal itself in your lifetime.

135. Don't pay any family member an executive salary for fulfilling a rank-and-file position.

136. Is the family wealth the golden goose or a golden calf?

You should be appropriately appreciative for the personal and financial opportunities afforded by wealth. You need to focus on the care and administration of the family's assets, which may have served one or more generations and should provide substantial financial benefits to future generations.

Families can, however, become obsessed with the source of

wealth. Initiated perhaps by only a few family members, this unhealthy preoccupation can be taught to younger generations. Don't let obsession become idol worship.

137. Consider writing an Ethical Will.

Ethical Wills are becoming increasingly popular as family leaders wish to pass down a legacy of values. You can memorialize your personal and spiritual beliefs, family history and culture, life lessons, and blessings for future generations.

138. One million dollars in cash is not equal to a one-million-dollar minority interest in a family-owned business.

THE REAL WORLD #1

Eighty-year-old Richard owned a well-known multistate business. Both his children worked with him. His son had the title of president but almost no authority. His daughter, an experienced certified public accountant, served as chief financial officer. His wife Doris was in poor health and rarely ventured outside the home.

Everyone in the company depended on Richard to make decisions—after all, building and running the company had dominated his entire life. But at last, Richard decided it might be time to discuss successorship and estate planning. In almost two years of meetings, he agonized over making even small gifts to his children and grandchildren, outright or in trust. He couldn't bring himself to think of retiring, or delegating all authority to his fifty-eight-year-old son.

His son had grown melancholy over the past ten or fifteen years after clinging to repeated promises that Dad would share equity in the company and, importantly, allow him to function as the real president. The daughter was content to do her job, but she had long given up trying to convince her father to invest in new technology and equipment to deal with accounts payable, accounts receivable, and shipping and receiving.

Epilogue: The company went downhill fast about this time. A new competitor—with new equipment, the latest technology, and enthusiastic employees—experienced dramatic growth at the expense of Richard's company. (Richard did not understand anything about computers or new technology, other than that it would "waste" a lot of money.)

Finally, at age sixty-two the son provoked a showdown with his father by announcing his retirement! His father was forced to sell a large portion of the company, and the son assumed control and ownership of a much smaller entity. Predictably, not a single grandchild chose to join the family business.

THE REAL WORLD #2

A third-generation family business had a reputation for making the best chili in the region. Numerous aunts, uncles, and cousins worked in the business. The restaurants were packed at lunchtime, dinner, and even in middle of the afternoon.

Much of the profits from the modestly successful business were reinvested to expand the first restaurant and eventually to add two locations.

Second-generation control ended with the death of two brothers, and stock was distributed widely among members of the third generation of the family. The company lacked leadership and direction, but was able to run as usual for five years or so. Over time, a number of the cousins chose other careers.

Some shareholders grumbled that the "valuable stock" should pay a dividend; others argued over the amount of compensation for family members active in the business. In an effort to make everyone happy, the company distributed a substantial portion of annual profits as dividends to the family owners. Little, if any, capital was used to upgrade and refurbish the restaurants.

The food was just as good and probably even more famous, but the restaurants changed from being quaint to being dumps. Though business—and profits—were flat for several years, many cousins had grown accustomed to their regular dividends and insisted that their dividend income could not be cut.

Epilogue: The restaurant and its famous name were sold to a group that included one branch of the family. It injected new capital into the company and stopped paying dividends. In a few years, the restaurants were regaining their popularity. The company trademarked the family name and licensed it to eager food manufacturers. The family business found new direction and prosperity, but only after acrimonious debate and dissention among the many cousins.

Professionally Speaking...

Many of our engagements involve a successful closely held business that is owned or controlled by a family group. Invariably, the key in providing help to these clients requires constructing an effective communication process within the family. Initially, we use exercises, small group discussions, questionnaires, and appropriate assessment tools to help family members discover the lack of good communication within the family group.

Next, we help family members separate family issues and dynamics from business issues and dynamics. We urge them to discuss emotion-based issues at home and make objective decisions at the business.

The final step is helping the family through the process of successorship.

Related axioms from Chapter 2

28. Maybe Junior doesn't want to run the family business. Can he tell you this without hurting you?

58. Don't pay a son a full-time salary from the business for a part-time effort.

59. Don't pay a daughter a salary from the business for staying home and raising your grandchildren.

Related axioms from Chapter 3

72. Why won't the old man let go of control—really?

73. Why won't the old man organize a board of directors for the family business—really?

75. Business successorship planning cannot be discussed until parents' financial security is successfully resolved.

76. Older family members have a natural aversion to debt.

Related axiom from Chapter 6

114. If an in-law is the best person to lead the family business or family financial matters, don't let fear of future divorce prevent the right choice.

8

Stewardship, Philanthropy, and Charitable Giving

Wealthy families have a greater opportunity, if not a greater responsibility, to include charitable gifts as an integral part of the financial planning process. At some point, you reach a limit on the level of satisfaction and happiness that wealth provides. Stewardship and philanthropy integrate well with the family values, goals, and morals you wish to pass on.

The qualitative attributes of charitable gifting are perhaps more important than the quantitative factors within the wealthy family. Make philanthropy and charitable giving a part of the overall financial planning process.

139. Children learn stewardship from observing their parents and other family members.

Move beyond tax incentives. You should have personal incentive to share a part of your wealth with the less-fortunate. Once you have all the expensive toys wealth can provide, and once you've provided long-term financial security for your family, turn your attention to sharing the excess. Learn to give to charity generously and with joy and enthusiasm.

If you find genuine joy in charitable giving, your children will learn the art of stewardship. Allow your children to share in your philanthropic endeavors. Talk with them about the decision-making behind distributing gifts and income from charitable trusts.

We all know money can buy an unlimited amount of material joy and satisfaction, but it cannot buy happiness. Stewardship and philanthropy may provide the key to true happiness, not only for you but for future generations of your family.

140. Let your child decide how to pass wealth along.

The majority of trusts pass a child's wealth on to his or her children at death. What about the child who has no children? Many trusts automatically transfer benefits to the other children and their issue. Rarely, a surviving spouse receives benefits.

Think about letting the child decide where the wealth goes upon his or her death. This gives them a chance to connect with other family members, an opportunity to say "thank you" to family members who have shown special care, love, and compassion.

141. If you intend to benefit charities in your will, find a way to do it while you are alive so you can derive joy and satisfaction from your gifts.

Many wealthy individuals tend to postpone acts of charity until death. On one hand, this preserves financial assets to assure long-term financial security. On the other hand, if you have more wealth than you'll need, you'll miss the joy of letting it work on behalf of your favorite causes while you're alive.

A qualified estate planner can explain options that can fulfill your personal financial goals, provide maximum tax benefits, and help the less-fortunate. Consider charitable remainder trusts, charitable lead trusts, gift annuities, and charitable gifting techniques that combine lifetime financial benefits with gifts to charity.

142. Philanthropy is the glue that binds generations of the family together.

Although love and affection reaches across generations, few activities can hold the interest of all. Administration of a family foundation or charitable trust, however, offers a rewarding and satisfying way to celebrate, and be grateful for, the opportunities afforded by wealth.

You'll teach younger family members the joys and responsibilities of stewardship. And you can maximize your tax advantages by doing something beneficial.

143. You are rich when you would rather give to charity than buy another toy.

Ellen Frankenberg, a well-known family business psychologist, coins the phrase "the joy to stuff ratio" in her book Your Family, Inc. Every wealthy family begins to receive less satisfaction from the accumulation of toys and luxuries. An excess of wealth can even lead to negativity and depression, as individuals learn first-hand that their money cannot buy happiness.

Explore the joy and satisfaction of charitable gifting when the emblems of wealthy living no longer provide heartfelt peace of mind. Make it a hobby to see how much in tax deductions you can generate through a careful plan of charitable giving.

---

144. You are rich when you successfully organize and operate a charitable foundation.

---

145. You are rich when you give it away with a smile.

145. You are rich when you give it away with a smile.

146. Advisors miss good opportunities to help wealthy clients learn the joys of charitable giving.

Wealthy individuals can be forgiven for not knowing all of the tax-related and emotional advantages of charitable giving, if they have not learned them from older family members. Yet professional advisors often fail to discuss charitable gifting options with wealthy clients unless prompted. They may think they're avoiding complications, controlling costs, or raising issues the client has not brought up. But most technical-based advisors don't recognize the importance of emotional factors within the family system. Be informed about the options. Talk about them.

147. Wealth is a shallow legacy without stewardship to address the needs of the poor.

148. Learn to be a philanthropist, or learn to ride a camel through the eye of a needle.

149. A family charitable lead trust creates the aura of wealth without boasting, the appearance of generous stewardship without facts and figures, and the actuality of tax savings and healthy training for children.

I've largely avoided technical topics in this book, but the charitable lead trust is an exception. Such trusts often work very well in the family financial plan, even without the tax savings granted by the IRS.

For example, well-to-do parents in their forties or fifties may make annual contributions of twenty thousand to fifty thousand dollars to an array of charitable organizations. They are not yet ready to make substantial gifts of assets to the children.

If the parents place four hundred thousand dollars of assets in a charitable lead trust (or a donor-advised fund with the local community foundation), they can make their regular charitable gifts out of this fund. After a fixed term of years, usually ten to fifteen years, whatever is left in the trust fund can then be distributed equally among the children.

They realize increased income tax benefits, applicable gift and estate tax savings, and the recognition associated with a family foundation. They provide peace of mind to their children— who know they will receive a significant amount at the end of the trust term— and teach them the lessons of stewardship in action.

THE REAL WORLD

Ron and Katherine, a couple in their seventies, have two terrific children, both married with families of their own. Ron worked in a factory all his life and lived on a small farm. He gradually began to accumulate modest rental homes and apartments in the area. Meanwhile, Katherine kept the books, dealt with tenants, collected the rent, and made mortgage payments to the bank.

They always lived very modestly and avoided taking any income from the rental operations. Almost without even realizing it, they accumulated a substantial net worth.

Ron was adamant that his wealth go to his children, either in the next several years or upon his death. He had no interest in discussion of charitable trusts or other similar planning tools.

Epilogue: Even after asking Ron what he would do with an extra million dollars—give an extra hundred thousand to his two children, or give the whole amount to charitable organizations—he insisted the money go to his children.

I called a family meeting to discuss a financial and estate plan for Ron, Katherine, and the children and grandchildren. Ron was surprised to hear his children, and their spouses, ask him to consider charitable gifts or charitable trusts as part of the plan.

The children were very comfortable financially;

they explained that it would be very hard to enjoy a lot of money in a small town. They insisted that their lives would be happier if Mom and Dad created a family foundation that the children and grandchildren could control for the benefit of charities and "good works" in the community.

Everybody cried, including me. Together, we had created a philanthropist!

Ron smiled a lot more in his final years. The family enjoyed getting together to consider gifts from the newly created family foundation. The grandchildren learned the joys of stewardship.

What a difference this plan made in the lives of the family and in their hometown.

Professionally Speaking...

We believe we have a commitment to help wealthy families explore the opportunities associated with charitable gifts, good works, and stewardship. Money cannot buy happiness, but perhaps giving it away can accomplish the goal.

We explain it like this: Suppose your four children will someday inherit one million dollars each from you. If you have an additional one million dollars, after taxes each child would inherit about fifty thousand dollars. Would you rather see the full million go to charitable organizations of your choice?

Similar planning opportunities are available for families with assets below the threshold for gift and estate taxes.

9

Investments and Finance

The responsibility of wealth usually includes management of substantial investment assets. Wealthy family members are obligated to learn as much as possible about finance, investments, and related matters. Even if they are not directly responsible for making decisions, they need enough knowledge to communicate effectively with the family's advisors.

And it's much easier to trust advisors when you understand what they're talking about.

150. Rich people don't balance their bank accounts: "Insufficient funds" means "out of checks."

151. Don't wait for a family crisis before thinking about long-term financial planning.

One reason people put off financial planning is not knowing where to start. Do you start with decisions about long-term healthcare or financial security during retirement years? Is protecting assets in a divorce more important than thinking about life insurance? Do we draw up a will first or finalize our financial plan? They think they have to think about everything and end up thinking about nothing.

The problem is that a list of issues is linear, but family planning is interrelated and co-dependent. Make a list of all your issues and concerns. Transfer your list to a circular chart. (See page 137.) Start anywhere, discuss the point, and follow its links around the circle. Try to understand each item before you begin thinking about decisions.

152. If investment managers (or anybody else) wants to run your family office "for free," start running.

153. Avoiding estate taxes is not the most important issue.

Don't make a financial plan designed only to minimize taxes. Each option involving special tax planning considerations should be carefully measured against personal and family objectives. Throw out any actions inconsistent with family culture, values, and desires.

154. Many family businesses will be sold for a lot of money some day; the beneficiaries often lack experience with financial and investment planning.

Wealthy family-business owners typically find almost their entire net worth invested in the enterprise. They have little experience investing liquid assets.

After selling the business, even a very successful owner may be lost when faced with managing the proceeds of the sale. Identify one or more "trusted advisors" to provide objective advice on developing a long-term investment plan.

155. Don't measure success in life by your annual financial statement—only the bank really cares about that.

---

156. When you plan your financial future, remember that life expectancy has increased by fourteen years in the past half century.

---

157. Take prudent steps to protect your assets.

---

158. Wealthy people pay more for products and services. Negotiate and shop around.

Store owners' eyes light up when an expensive car drives up. Service workers add a surcharge when they see your fancy house.

What's worse, many wealthy individuals disdain the "unpleasantness" of negotiating prices. If you are personally uncomfortable with discussing prices for products and services, consider engaging an advisor to do the dirty work.

And remember, you may not be paying higher prices just because you're rich. Ask yourself if you're very particular about results or demand perfect service: You may need to expect to pay a premium price for being hard to work with.

158. Wealthy people pay more for products and services. Negotiate and shop around.

159. Beware of inherent, and possibly subtle, conflicts of interest when your accountant or financial advisor also provides ancillary business services and financial products.

People expect financial advisors to render competent advice and rarely seek a second opinion, even if they are unfamiliar with the jargon or technical aspects of the field. But it's unreasonable to expect your advisor not to have some degree of bias toward products and financial service packages in which he or she has a personal financial interest. It is simply human nature that quickly works to your disadvantage.

---

160. Even if you can afford a second home at the beach, why not just rent a property when you want to go on vacation?

THE REAL WORLD

Ben and Susan are in their sixties, with three children and eleven grandchildren. They have substantial assets, more than they need for financial security and long-term care when they retire. They have had excellent investment advice and created a solid estate plan carried out through a good set of wills. But their simple plan will eventually result in substantial gift or estate taxes, which could easily be avoided.

They have issues:

"We want to provide financial benefits to our children, and save future gift/estate taxes, without worrying about our children's inexperience in handling money."

"Our son is a doctor who may lose everything in a malpractice suit, and our second daughter is a spendthrift and always overdrawn at the bank."

"I need all of my money for long-term healthcare; my wealth is only enough for my financial security."

"I would do anything for the children if we had another five hundred thousand dollars."

"We want to encourage our children to have a good work ethic, so we don't want them to have a lot of money."

Epilogue: Many of our clients turn to us after developing a plan with another professional. Ben and Susan may have shared their concerns, but what they say initially is not always the whole truth. Behind their stated issues is a hidden agenda. In this case, they're concerned about the stability of one child's marriage. They simply cannot talk about this. The daughter is already angry, and they fear the truth will ruin their relationship with their grandchildren.

They must talk candidly about the issues before we can help them choose tools and techniques to address their concerns. The worst thing parents can do is to avoid the planning process altogether; children can see right through lame excuses.

If they don't talk it out, the parents' fear about a child's marriage may eventually be resolved, only to be replaced by a new issue—and another excuse to avoid the planning process.

Professionally Speaking…

This is the most important lesson in this book.

We typically ask family members to make a list of specific concerns and issues, which we transfer to a circular chart. They find it much easier to understand how each item interrelates. (See Figures B, C, and D.) Remember, the order of the items should be random in nature, and it makes no difference where you begin discussions.

As you work through the circular discussion, you will invariably come across one item the family won't discuss—though the issue is different for every family. It's taboo, and they've secretly agreed not to discuss it because it's painful to think about, too hurtful to talk about. It probably involves deep emotional conflict or even mental illness. You can recommend getting help from a psychologist, psychiatrist, or family relationship consultant, but the family probably won't accept the idea at this time.

You need to be circumspect. Build a bridge over this topic, put a Band-aid on it, put a fence around it, or just skip it. Get by it, go around it, or move quickly past it. But under no circumstances should you allow this hot topic to stymie the planning process.

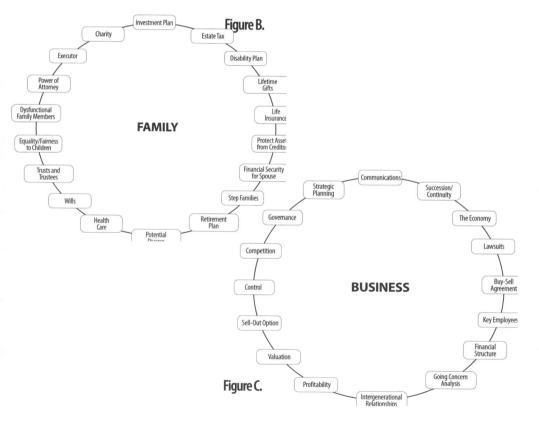

The issues are inter-related and discussion seems to go around in a circle—solutions to individual prolems are elusive. Break the circle at any point to begin the problem-solving process.

It's just not fair to the family for issues associated with one member to overwhelm the needs of the others. Even if an in-law is a rotten scoundrel or one child's a felon or a sibling is mentally ill, this cannot be an excuse to avoid financial planning.

If you're not careful, this topic can derail the entire planning process.

My experience invariably has been that working around the hot topic allows the family to resolve many other issues overshadowed by the single factor. After family members have developed a plan that allows each of them to move forward, then it is much easier for them to focus on that single unresolved issue.

At this point, family members might be receptive to professional help.

Figure D.

Related axiom from Chapter 1

7. Accept the responsibility to learn about raising wealthy children—do not try to make it up as you go.

Related axioms from Chapter 2

35. Be suspicious if your child does not believe in prenuptial agreements.

43. Any of your children can run a valuable, low-debt business (into the ground.

Related axioms from Chapter 3

74. The greatest loss of wealth occurs when the person controlling it fails to identify his or her own senility, dementia, or other mental impairment.

75. Business successorship planning cannot be discussed until parents' financial security is successfully resolved.

76. Older family members have a natural aversion to debt.

Related axioms from Chapter 5

98. "The bank did a terrible job with my mother's trust." When you hear this, remember there are two sides to the story.

99. "The stupid bank 'sits on' the trust my parents established for me, and I get almost nothing out of it." Remember, that's why the parents put wealth in trust in the first place.

100. "Because of the stupid bank, my trust has not grown at all in twenty years."

Related axioms from Chapter 7

116. Selling the family business may be the best option. Move your legacy to another memorial site.

126. Conduct an emergency fire drill; what will happen if you die or become incapacitated today?

138. One million dollars in cash is not equal to a one-million-dollar minority interest in a family-owned business.

10

Wills and Estate Planning

None of us likes to contemplate our own death, so we put off planning our estates. People who create the wealth want to hang onto it until death; people who inherit their wealth often have the same desire.

These attitudes are short-sighted and irresponsible in the context of the family group. You'll benefit far more from sharing the enjoyment of your wealth, and you'll live long enough to benefit two or three generations of the family.

You may be more comfortable thinking about life planning instead of estate planning. The most attractive options in a long-term plan of asset distribution require action years before you die. Gift planning, charitable planning, financial planning, trusts for family members, and minimization of future taxes must all be a part of any comprehensive planning process.

161. Family limited partnerships are good estate planning devices, but they may not be good for your family.

Lawyers, accountants, and other financial planners frequently make the mistake of focusing on the tantalizing challenge of minimizing potential taxes. Accounting gimmicks take precedence over the family's best interests. And too many professional advisors limit their scope to technical issues without concern for the family side of estate planning.

Your advisors need to find out if the family wants a partnership to share ownership of significant financial assets. They need to make sure all family members are comfortable that only a few family members will make the decisions. They need to address differences in financial circumstances between different family groups. And they need to balance the family's goals: Some will want to retain assets for future generations, while others will want to sell assets for the current generation.

162. Too much focus and attention is placed on "Mr. Big."

Professional service providers and business consultants make a mistake when they focus overwhelming attention on the one who holds control over the family wealth—especially if Mr. Big has attained near-celebrity status. This gives the other family members the uneasy feeling that the advisors are trying to please only the family member with the most influence over decision-making. When most of the attention is focused on Mr. Big, family members think that their interests and concerns are less significant in the decision-making process.

Smart advisors understand that the majority of goals and objectives of the planning process pertain to conditions after Mr. Big is dead or disabled. It is vital that they involve the other family members to determine *their* objectives.

In fact, Mr. Big himself is probably in the best position to balance the communication process and make sure the entire family group participates. This may be why Craig Aronoff and John Ward describe the act of successorship as "the final act of greatness." (See Axiom 4.)

163. There is no such thing as a simple will.

Don't try to save time and money by executing a simple will. You may wish to avoid contemplating your mortality. You may not want to relinquish your power and control. But you need to develop a good will for your spouse and children, not for you—because you're dead. Assume the responsibility that accompanies your wealth; you're selfish to place loved ones in jeopardy because you insist on a "simple will."

162. Too much focus and attention is placed on "Mr. Big."

164. Negative thoughts lead to shutdown in the planning process.

165. Some accountants and lawyers let their clients make decisions without learning the basic facts.

When wealthy clients consult a professional advisor about an estate plan, they typically have given some thought to their goals and objectives. They may have developed a list of specific actions.

You do yourself a disservice by not taking advantage of your advisor's experience and expertise. Don't make decisions when you aren't even aware of all the options.

An experienced estate planner should insist the client explore all of the alternatives before making a decision.

166. Discussion is difficult because many issues overlap and are interdependent.

Dealing with multiple issues would be much easier if each problem could be put on a checklist and resolved one after another. Wealth planning would be like grocery shopping—grabbing solutions off the shelves one by one.

But planning issues are not isolated. They have vague, overlapping boundaries; they reflect interdependent and dynamic relationships. Discussing and resolving any one issue impacts previously settled decisions and issues that haven't even come up yet.

165. Some accountants and lawyers let their clients make decisions without learning the basic facts.

One approach is to identify each issue, arrange them in a random circle, and randomly choose one topic. (See page 136.) The group then moves around the circle in a fluid, flexible discussion. After everyone understands each issue and its relation to the others, they make a second trip around the circle to make decisions.

167. Does your lawyer recognize, appreciate, and prioritize the human side of estate planning?

THE REAL WORLD

Claude and Diane are a well-to-do couple in their mid-sixties. They have a typical assortment of children and grandchildren with happy, healthy, and productive lives. Claude is the successful chief executive officer of a local subsidiary of a publicly owned company.

Claude didn't think it was important for his wife to attend meetings on estate planning. He designed his own plan and dominated the discussions. He wanted Diane to be well cared for if she survived him, and he was certain that she would be "much better off" if the bank served as trustee for investment and administration of the family assets.

Diane suggested that she would like to understand the role of the trustee in providing for her financial security. Claude insisted that a marital trust and family trust was the right plan for Diane and the family. Only their home was held jointly; it would belong to Diane outright after Claude died. Even a substantial retirement account was payable to a special trust created under Claude's will.

Epilogue: After Claude died, Diane surprised everyone by electing against the will even though she was the beneficiary of a large trust. She received substantial assets, outright and free of trust, and the remaining assets were held in trust for the benefit of her children.

Diane was bitter and frustrated with her husband's over-protective attitude. She had always longed to control her own, unrestricted assets. But, she said with exasperation, there was no sense trying to argue with Claude while he was alive.

Claude's estate plan did not survive him.

Professionally Speaking...

In our practice, we make an effort to emphasize equal care, concern, and attention for both spouses.

In many cases, the husband is the dominant member of the family and controller of its assets. He is usually a leader accustomed to a great deal of attention from employees, vendors, and advisors. The wife, on the other hand, may be resigned to sitting on the sideline while her husband engages in financial and estate planning for both of them.

We insist on using a round table for our family meetings in order to emphasize the equal importance of each family member, including children.

Related axioms from Chapter 1

3. Financial planning for the family is pointless until absolute financial security is assured for Mom.

14. Don't use wealth to control family members from the grave.

15. Rich parents should not try to use wealth to control, direct, or influence decisions that children need to make for themselves.

Related axioms from Chapter 2

25. Special children (disabled, chemically dependent, emotionally unstable) need compassion—and special trust provisions.

32. Rich fathers will struggle to balance financial benefits for two sets of children if they don't communicate with everybody.

34. Have your estate sale now, and prevent World War III from breaking out at your death.

39. It is impossible to treat all children equally, so stop trying.

40. Is equal really fair?

41. Many wealthy families allow one dysfunctional child to stymie the planning process for the entire family.

42. You are truly wealthy when you are concerned about leaving too much to the kids.

Related axiom from Chapter 3

72. Why won't the old man "let go" of control—really?

Related axiom from Chapter 4

85. A postnuptial agreement can protect assets for the children, regardless of future actions by the survivor.

Related axiom from Chapter 5

88. Rich parents are reluctant to transfer wealth to their children for fear much will be lost in a divorce.

102. There is no such thing as a simple trust.

104. Trusts that pay only income for the life of a beneficiary may not be wise.

Related axiom from Chapter 6

115. Two spouses in a second marriage create a disaster for the family of the first spouse to die by trying to share a simple estate plan.

Related axioms from Chapter 7

119. Successorship is a process, not an event.

120. Successorship will be decided in the limousines during your funeral procession if you don't do it beforehand.

121. You can't select a successor by flipping a coin on your deathbed.

123. It is better to accept the fact that issues are interrelated in a circle than to struggle down a spiral staircase.

126. Conduct an emergency fire drill; what will happen if you die or become incapacitated today?

127. Consider dictating your hopes, beliefs, wishes, thoughts, and suggestions for the family and the business after your death or incapacity.

128. The time, effort, and expense of strategic family business planning greatly increases the odds of success.

129. Be suspicious when a family member insists that he or she must have fifty-one percent of the voting power.

132. Why do people with power, money, and control try to make decisions without knowing all the facts, alternatives, and lessons from others?

133. The golden goose that produces bounty for only one master will be divided into many parts at the master's death.

134. You can face your own mortality if you can voluntarily surrender power, money, and control to your successors.

138. One million dollars in cash is not equal to a one-million-dollar minority interest in a family-owned business.

Related axioms from Chapter 8

140. Let your child decide how to pass wealth along.

141. If you intend to benefit charities in your will, find a way to do it while you are alive so you can derive joy and satisfaction from your gifts.

Related axioms from Chapter 9

151. Don't wait for a family crisis before thinking about long-term financial planning.

153. Avoiding estate taxes is not the most important issue.

11

Lawyers and Other Advisors

Most family members will concede that outside professional expertise and advice is extremely important for the accumulation, preservation, enjoyment, and distribution of wealth. But there's always one who argues against it, usually on the basis of cost, time, perceived conflicts of interest, or thinking they know everything one needs to know about the subject.

Professional advisors will more than pay for themselves by increasing wealth, increasing income from wealth, minimizing taxes, and cutting costs. Regardless of the money, however, you can justify the cost of outside professional advice because of the feelings of financial security, fiscal safety, and reduced stress you receive.

And you'll realize significant value because your advisor will educate your children and other family members about the issues and problems of wealth. You'll be able to delegate responsibilities to professional advisors so that your family can spend its time actually enjoying the benefits of wealth.

Professional advisors also offer objective and competent service for elderly or disabled family members, who may otherwise be caught between well-meaning family members with differing opinions.

Clearly, wealthy families can afford qualified professional advice. But they may have trouble identifying and appreciating the need for it.

Multidisciplinary "trusted advisors" are essential. They must be able to balance complexly intertwined issues of business and family. Otherwise, they can do only half the job.

Wealthy families naturally invest a great deal of trust in lawyers because of their training, experience, their obligation to confidentiality, and their strict ethical rules. You need to identify the right lawyer for your team of professional advisors. Litigators and divorce lawyers may be disqualified by their win-at-all-costs, us-versus-them attitudes. The skills of real estate or corporate lawyers may be too limited for broad family planning.

Families need lawyers who appreciate mediation, facilitation, intermediation, win/win outcomes, compassion, and the dynamics of family systems. You can easily buy technical expertise, but it is much more difficult to identify advisors who will work with family members to explore alternatives, consider options, and work together in family meetings.

168. Do not automatically run away from life insurance professionals.

Life insurance almost always plays a valuable role in the financial plan.

169. Make sure you have the right property and casualty insurance on the right assets, in the right amounts, and for the right risks.

Get competent, objective advice before trouble strikes.

170. Make sure you have the right comprehensive liability insurance in the right amounts, and for the right risks. Get competent, objective advice before trouble strikes.

Wealthy individuals are easy targets for frivolous lawsuits. Some people think they've won the lottery when they have an accident involving the vehicle or property of a wealthy person. And your lawyer will probably recommend even a substantial settlement over risking a jury's prejudices against the wealthy and for the less-fortunate.

Don't wait until someone files a claim before reading your liability insurance policy. You can get large amounts of coverage at a relatively small cost covering a number of loss contingencies.

Obtain advice from a liability insurance specialist who works with other wealthy families. They will read the list of exclusions as carefully as they read the list of covered events.

171. Don't pick your advisors by throwing darts. Do your homework in advance.

You will find professional advisors with excellent technical skills and experience if you do your homework. Use interviews, referrals, investigations, and discreet inquiries to pick the best candidates from the field of lawyers, accountants, financial planners, insurance professionals, and other advisors. Remember, you're hiring an individual, not his or her highly respected firm.

Discover how your potential advisors think about the human side of planning. A candidate quick to offer a standard set of plans

171. Don't pick your advisors by throwing darts. Do your homework in advance.

at an attractive price may not embrace the important dynamics of the family system.

You must take the initiative and make sure any planner addresses non-technical issues. Saving on taxes and creating an estate plan at the lowest cost are not the highest priorities for wealthy families.

172. When interviewing professional advisors, look for family pictures rather than college degrees and awards.

Be cautious about relying on advice from friends and relatives. Scrutinize their qualifications as closely you would an outsider. And remember, it is much easier to reprimand, fire, or even sue an outside party.

173. Trusted advisors can provide valuable objective and unemotional advice.

Seeking advice from a qualified family member is tempting. You have to trust your professional advisor, and a family member provides an extra measure of comfort. But a family member may lack objectivity, subtly injecting your plan with their own opinions and attitudes.

And it's easy to misread a family member's level of experience and expertise. Your son-in-law may be a fine young man, a wonderful husband to your daughter and father to your grandchildren, but is he qualified to guide you through the important process of planning for your family?

174. Outside facilitators will both manage and enhance the family communication process.

Don't rely on each other to conduct the discussions within the family group, especially when multiple generations are involved. Outside facilitators have multidisciplinary training in socio-psychological principles, behavioral organizational sciences, and related skills. Look for holistic advisors, comfortable with both the technical aspects of finance, accounting, and law and the emotional aspects of human interaction.

175. Can your lawyer use the L word without a silly grin?

As a group, lawyers are extremely bright, talented and hard working, tenacious and argumentative, willing to win by using the smallest technical loophole.

None of these talents demonstrates that they appreciate and understand the human side of estate planning. Can your lawyer differentiate between technical issues of the business system and the emotionally based issues of the family system? You may need to keep looking until you find a lawyer who can use the word "love" without smirking.

THE REAL WORLD

Bill, the founder and president of a publicly traded company, contemplated retirement in a year or two. He was ready to think about financial, retirement, tax, and estate planning.

Bill had a relatively new wife, several children, and numerous grandchildren. The children have multiple divorces and remarriages. They possess modest means, in contrast to their father's substantial assets.

In my initial interview with Bill, he showed me a stack of extensive proposals created by five well-known financial and investment planning organizations. We reviewed the principal recommendations from each advisor; not surprisingly, they were all very similar. Bill asked me which plan I favored.

Epilogue: I refused to give him any advice until I had a better understanding of his objectives for himself, his wife, his children, and even his grandchildren. I told him, "Even plans with significant financial or tax advantages are undesirable if they fail to address specific needs and goals for you and your family."

Then and there, Bill decided to start over with his planning process. I spent two months conducting intimate interviews with Bill, his wife, and each of his children and their spouses. Only then did we begin to analyze specific tools and alternatives for building their comprehensive financial plan.

Professionally Speaking ...

Thousands of professional advisors compete for the opportunity to assist wealthy families with the administration and distribution of assets. Technical-based professionals such as lawyers, accountants, and financial advisors place far too much attention on these assets, which fit the "comfort zone" of many family members, especially the men.

The successful professional advisor, however, should focus first on family-related issues. You can't devise a plan for managing and distributing assets without analyzing the personal goals of the family. By focusing on their needs, you also gain their confidence and build their trust for your plan. The family-based approach can give you a key competitive edge.

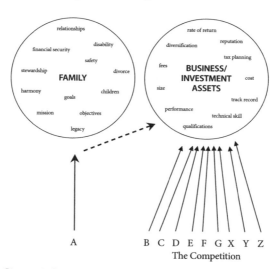

Figure E. You can flip a coin between B through Z. Who will stand out as special and unique in proposing a relationship? Who will be differentiated from the competition? Who will earn the coveted role of "trusted advisor"? The family business or investment plan must address and integrate family system goals and issues in development of a comprehensive and holistic plan of action.

Related axiom from Chapter 8

146. Advisors miss good opportunities to help wealthy clients learn the joys of charitable giving.

Related axioms from Chapter 9

152. If investment managers (or anybody else) wants to run your family office "for free," start running.

154. Many family businesses will be sold for a lot of money some day; the beneficiaries often lack experience with financial and investment planning.

159. Beware of inherent, and possibly subtle, conflicts of interest when your accountant or financial advisor also provides ancillary business services and financial products.

Related axioms from Chapter 10

162. Too much focus and attention is placed on "Mr. Big."

165. Some accountants and lawyers let their clients make decisions without learning the facts.

167. Does your lawyer recognize, appreciate, and prioritize the human side of estate planning?

Inheritance

The challenges confronting inheritors are unique and often misunderstood. Many observers wonder, "How can anyone with so much money not be happy?"

In truth, inheriting wealth has its own special burdens. Inheritors lack the satisfaction of earning wealth, and face unexpected issues of stewardship and responsibility. Their role in the family, and in society, changes dramatically.

Inherited wealth is a blessing, but without care it can become a curse.

176. Inherited wealth is often mistaken for earned success, which can create emotional problems for inheritors seeking normalcy.

In the beginning, most inheritors are enthusiastic and grateful about their sudden wealth, even if they've been expecting it. They soon find out they're facing significant changes in life—including new duties and responsibilities—and in lifestyle.

Long-time friends may become jealous and distance themselves. People at work may no longer respect your hard work. Family members who did not share in the windfall may view you in a different light. Representatives of charitable organizations will ask you to join their boards—and contribute your money.

Inheritors often try to prove they deserve such a windfall by making generous contributions to charities and by sharing financial benefits with family members.

The key may be for an inheritor to make gradual changes in lifestyle, or none at all.

177. The satisfaction and joy of building wealth is much different from the satisfaction and joy of inheriting it.

In today's economy wealth can be earned almost as quickly as it can be inherited. Even so, it still takes hard work to earn a fortune, which creates a special sense of satisfaction.

Inheritors must find a different reward. They can use the windfall gift to create greater wealth through earnings and per-

176. Inherited wealth is often mistaken for earned success, which can create emotional problems for inheritors seeking normalcy.

sonal efforts. They can support good works by endowing charitable organizations. They can create a legacy by teaching their children good stewardship.

---

178. A sudden change from non-wealth to wealth will disrupt some family relationships. Be prepared, be sensitive, and be patient.

---

179. Do not give an inheritance with unnecessary strings attached.

Too often, parents and other senior family members are tempted to include formal or informal limitations on a gift or inheritance. Formal provisions may be drafted into a trust document; more often parents communicate their restrictions informally, saying "do not ever sell the family farm" or "this should be a gift that you should enjoy for your lifetime and then give to your oldest son."

Such restrictions usually reflect the parents' current situation, thoughts, and emotions, ignoring the long-term effects on the family's assets.

Here's some blunt advice: If you are going to give a gift, then give it outright and unconditionally. Get a professional's advice if you think there are strong extenuating circumstances.

180. If you receive a substantial gift or inheritance, make sure you clearly communicate with the donor about any formal or informal restrictions attached.

Gift recipients and inheritors should not be left to wonder whether it is okay to sell a substantial asset. With the wealth comes a responsibility to understand any restrictions on its use and enjoyment.

The general rule is to avoid implied restrictions or limitations. The donor should spell out any restrictions. Tell them: "Yes, it is okay to sell this asset or give it to charity." The recipient should be very careful not to assume implied limitations. And recipients should never transfer usch assumptions to members of the next generation, which will only compound frustrations and potential problems within the family.

THE REAL WORLD

Janice is in her mid-forties with a good husband and wonderful children. She owns a one-fourth interest in her grandfather's successful company and recently began receiving substantial cash distributions every year. She has two million dollars in a separate bank account in her name, and expects millions more in the future.

Except for paying income taxes, Janice refuses to touch these funds for any reason. She plans to accumulate the funds and bequeath the wealth to her children equally. She says this is what her grandfather and her dead mother would expect of her. Only her husband and income tax preparer are aware of her substantial assets.

Janice suffered a mental breakdown recently, surprising her friends and relatives. The burden of her inheritance had become too much to bear.

Epilogue: Good financial planning and family communication could have made her inheritance a wonderful gift and opportunity. Instead, Janice is in therapy, and she has exciting plans for her substantial assets when she recovers. For now, her wealth is held in a money market fund account yielding one percent annual interest.

Professionally Speaking...

As we talk candidly with individuals who inherited their wealth, we see their burdens and concerns. In many cases, guilt causes a wealthy inheritor to do nothing with the assets except enjoy the income and pass the wealth to the next generation at death. Survivors whose wealth comes from the family of the deceased spouse have a particularly difficult time.

We try to help inheritors identify personal goals that will make them happy and keep them going forward in life. Professional advisors should be sensitive to negative attitudes that need to be rechanneled into opportunities. Wealth that sits passively will never challenge and stimulate its beneficiaries.

Related axioms from Chapter 2

26. Use trust funds to support children who work for other reasons than money.

31. Children, ignore your parents at your peril—emotional balance is more important than your share of the inheritance.

34. Have your estate sale now, and prevent World War III from breaking out at your death.

42. You are truly wealthy when you are concerned about leaving too much to the kids.

54. To the Next Generation: "Are you ready, today, to accept responsibility for assets and wealth?"

Related axioms from Chapter 3

64. How does it happen that a rich widow gets control of the family business at her husband's death? And does she really want it?

75. Business successorship planning cannot be discussed until parents' financial security is successfully resolved.

Related axioms from Chapter 5

99. "The stupid bank 'sits on' the trust my parents established for me, and I get almost nothing out of it." Remember, that's why the parents put wealth in trust in the first place.

101. Why do some wealthy parents prefer trusts for daughters, but not for sons—really?

103. The promise of annual financial support can never take the place of a trust or annuity.

104. Trusts that pay only income for the life of a beneficiary may not be wise.

Related axioms from Chapter 9

154. Many family businesses will be sold for a lot of money some day; the beneficiaries often lack experience with financial and investment planning.

156. When you plan your financial future, remember that life expectancy has increased by fourteen years in the past half century.

13

Family Offices, Retreats, and Councils

When wealth is shared by more than one family unit across several generations, the family needs systems to coordinate the enjoyment and responsibilities of wealth.

The family office can streamline communications and cut costs; today's version of the family office can provide business services for a hundred or more family members.

The family council comprises family members with a full range of academic, mental, and business talents and acumen. Every family member from adolescents to the reigning patriarchs and matriarchs should actively participate in family retreats and family council meetings.

Senior family members can use a family retreat to express their ideas and concerns about passing on ownership of family assets. Other family members have their own agendas; everybody must have an adequate opportunity to be heard and understood. Issues over shared legacies often stem from the lack of time and opportunity for good communication.

All of these systems encourage open communication and better financial management.

181. The family office should do a lot more than balance the household checkbooks.

The traditional family office supplied accounting and secretarial services to handle financial matters and personal affairs for the boss's family. Today's family office offers fifty or more personal and business services for an entire family unit spanning several generations.

182. The family office should be separate from the family business.

A separate office is more flexible, has fewer entanglements, and will survive the sale of the family company.

183. Family councils, family retreats, and family offices greatly aid the process of determining successorship and building a legacy.

Wealthy families need an organizational structure and governance system to ensure responsible and efficient administration of family business interests and investments. Usually, family members with expertise and interest in the administration of wealth work together as the elected members of the family council. Governance should be democratic with regular elections and rotation of responsibilities among family members and, perhaps, professional advisors.

Non-active family members should expect their interests to be represented fairly and equally within the family council in return for relinquishing their influence.

Family retreats, on the other hand, should be broadly inclusive, similar to open shareholder meetings. They serve as a forum for dissemination of information about family matters and education about the family legacy and history.

184. Separate leadership of the family council from leadership of the family business.

Some heads of the family enterprises—the leader of the family business or the ones who manage the assets—automatically assume the mantle of leadership in the family itself. But well-managed families appreciate the need to separate family leadership from family business leadership.

Sharing leadership encourages more family members to participate, offering different perspectives and representing more interests. It helps the family maintain checks and balances in decision-making. And getting more people involved keeps the family council process from suffering because of inaction and apathy.

185. Try converting family reunions into family retreats that combine business with pleasure.

If you've never convened a family council, you may experience some resistance to the project from family members unfamiliar or uncomfortable with the concept. Consider incorporating the discussions into a family reunion.

This plan gives everyone a chance to renew old relationships, meet new family members, and strengthen family ties before getting down to business.

THE REAL WORLD

A third-generation family collectively controlled a publicly traded manufacturing company. The president of the company, David, foresaw the dilution of the family's power as older family members died, resulting in a wide dispersion of stock among a large number of cousins scattered from coast to coast.

David, together with his high-priced lawyer and accountant, organized a family meeting for more than forty family members. The various family branches gathered for a happy reunion—a time for sharing ideas, celebrating their legacy, and making important decisions for the future.

Epilogue: Unfortunately David, an industry giant earning nearly two million dollars a year, made obvious mistakes at the meeting.

He thought he was being subtle as he tried convincing family members to transfer their voting stock to a voting trust. (He, of course, volunteered to be the trustee, for the benefit of all family members.)

He organized a tight agenda that gave little opportunity for other family members to express their opinions.

He presented the plan prepared by accountants and lawyers and asked for a vote.

His plan never even made it to the floor for a vote. And the family won't have another meeting for years.

Professionally Speaking ...

Many families underestimate the importance of a family meeting or retreat to discuss financial assets and the family-owned business. Typically, the family has one or two successful business people or professionals who think that they can organize and lead the family through such a meeting. They end up doing a poor job of hiding their personal biases and objectives; this makes other family members determined to resist their clumsy efforts.

Professional advisors perform a valuable role in facilitating the family's communication process.

Related axiom from Chapter 7

130. Do not use a family council to control family members.

14

Family Legacy and Family Values

Its legacy and values are the essence of a family. A family legacy comprises material wealth, businesses and foundations, celebrations and celebrities, memories, stories, and even legends. This legacy can be a golden goose or a golden calf, proudly celebrated or falsely worshipped.

Family values represent important behaviors, idiosyncrasies, beliefs, goals, and morals common to a specific family group. Values define a family group just as dollar signs measure a family's wealth; without one, the other is worthless.

186. The golden goose will not long reside in a family bereft of good values and high morals.

187. Keep the family album up to date; it's an important part of your legacy. Include everyone regardless of stature, wealth, or success.

Families with one or two particularly successful or wealthy members tend to focus far too much attention on them. It's natural to celebrate their success, but the family system inherently treats all family members equally, regardless of celebrity, wealth, or social status.

Younger family members in particular will pick up on an imbalance of attention in the family album. Make sure everyone is represented, and celebrated.

188. Conspicuous consumption does not demonstrate real wealth.

Who's wealthier, the person who earns a lot of money and spends it all, or the couple living a simple life on their five-hundred-acre farm?

Stately mansions, beach houses, and expensive cars don't demonstrate wealth. Look at the values being taught to the children in these disparate families. When each set of children gains control over the wealth, their balance sheets may look the same, but their values will determine the family legacy.

187. Keep the family album up to date; it's an important part of your legacy. Include everyone regardless of stature, wealth, or success.

189. Families that work together need lives of their own.

Sometimes the individual is lost as multi-generational family groups celebrate a common legacy in family meetings or the family business. Each family unit comprises values and relationships that are a composite of two or more senior members. These new family units need permission, time, and space to explore, develop, and enjoy creating their own new legacy.

190. Do not allow family traditions and gatherings to prevent children from developing a healthy degree of independence with his or her own family.

Strong, close-knit families enjoy time together. But reunions, family meetings, joint vacations, birthdays, anniversaries, funerals, weddings, and graduations can quickly fill the calendar. As families grow and age, even more gatherings join the list. And no one ever cancels a traditional celebration. This leaves little time for individual families to develop and enjoy their own traditions and celebrations apart from the larger group.

In-laws are a complicating factor. Remember, younger family members share the blood and traditions of two families—not just yours. They need equal time to cultivate relationships in the other family. And they need time to create their own traditions, to shape their own lives and those of their spouses and children.

Never let a celebration become an obligation.

191. It is possible to transfer the family legacy from one asset to another without diminishing the joy of common family ownership.

The idea of selling a long-time family business or homeplace can be devastating. The ghosts of long-dead family members become vivid and real, conjuring up fears of guilt and retribution.

But sometimes circumstances necessitate selling the core of the family legacy. The best way to deal with the grief and betrayal associated with the sale is to transfer the family's emotional ties to another asset or undertaking. Consider creating a charitable foundation, a new family legacy controlled by a broad group of family members. Consider writing an Ethical Will. (See axiom 137.)

THE REAL WORLD

Jack and Ann are a wonderful couple in their late thirties with three beautiful and healthy children. Jack is a successful doctor.

The family lives hundreds of miles away from Ann's well-to-do family and from Jack's upper-middle-class family.

Ann's childhood was filled with family traditions centering around birthdays, weddings, anniversaries, and holidays, many started by her grandparents and continuing today.

Eventually, moving back to Ann's hometown became less problematic than traveling back and forth. Now Jack and Ann, and, most importantly, their children, can participate in all of the family's get-togethers and traditions.

Epilogue: As Jack and Ann teach their children the rich traditions of Ann's family, they need also to be mindful of leaving ample time to interact with Jack's family. If they don't, they run the risk of making the other side of the family resentful. The grandchildren will be much closer to her parents than his. At the same time, Jack and Ann need to establish boundaries of independence for their immediate family as a separate unit enjoying its own traditions.

Professionally Speaking ...

As we help multiple family units organize ways to honor the family legacy, we also encourage individual family members to make a healthy separation from the family group.

Each family member must find a different balance between his or her original family and the new family created through marriage.

There is not a choice between parents and siblings or spouse and children. There is only balance, good or bad.

Related axioms from Chapter 1

4. A father must "anoint" his son as his final act of greatness.

5. A mother must let go of her child as her final act of greatness.

6. A father must respect his daughter as an independent young adult.

17. The most joyful and satisfying hobby in later life is watching your children become young adults—serving as your successors and preserving your legacy—after you relinquish power, money, and control.

Related axioms from Chapter 2

1. If rich children rarely interact with regular folks, how can they interact with the real world later in life?

31. Children, ignore your parents at your peril—emotional balance is more important than your share of the inheritance.

22. If your children attend elite private schools, make opportunities for them to interact in the real world that includes non-rich people and persons of different ethnic and cultural backgrounds.

23. Observe how your children treat the maid, the landscaper, the delivery man, the plumber, the repairman, the school teacher, the secretary, the waitress, the store clerk, and the salesperson.

35. Be suspicious if your child does not believe in prenuptial agreements.

38. Work to transfer family values along with family wealth.

42. You are truly wealthy when you are concerned about leaving too much to the kids.

45. Sometimes, a child and his or her spouse need to start their own family legacy.

Related axiom from Chapter 3

64. How does it happen that a rich widow gets control of the family business at her husband's death? And does she really want it?

Related axiom from Chapter 4

85. A postnuptial agreement can protect assets for the children, regardless of future actions by the survivor.

Related axiom from Chapter 5

101. Why do some wealthy parents prefer trusts for daughters, but not for sons—really?

Related axioms from Chapter 6

111. You are rich when you love your in-laws and they love you.

112. Ignore your in-laws at your peril.

Related axioms from Chapter 7

116. Selling the family business may be the best option. Move your legacy to another memorial site.

120. Successorship will be decided in the limousines during your funeral procession if you don't do it beforehand.

121. You can't select a successor by flipping a coin on your deathbed.

125. If neglected, abused, or taken for granted, a golden goose can slowly die from a broken heart.

136. Is the family wealth the golden goose or a golden calf?

137. Family history, culture, and values greatly impact family business ownership and management.

Related axioms from Chapter 8

139. Children learn stewardship from observing their parents and other family members.

143. You are rich when you would rather give to charity than buy another toy.

145. You are rich when you give it away with a smile.

147. Wealth is a shallow legacy without stewardship to address the needs of the poor.

148. Learn to be a philanthropist, or learn to ride a camel through the eye of a needle.

Related link from Chapter 12

176. Inherited wealth is often mistaken for earned success, which can create emotional problems for inheritors seeking normalcy.

15

Communicating Family Systems Issues

This chapter covers family themes associated with psychology, sociology, and behavioral sciences, including conflict, men versus woman, wealth sucessorship, and shared ownership.

The family system, and its specific problems and issues, deserves special treatment.

In many cases, qualified professional advice is necessary to facilitate exploration of these issues. Importantly, having outside professionals facilitate the process can help members of a family group more comfortably discuss issues and reach their own decisions. Families do not need professional advisors to tell them what to do. Families only need guidance through the communication process to find the answers and to develop their strategic plan.

192. A detailed graph of the psychological family tree reveals the motivations of individual family members.

A trained family systems therapist or family relationship consultant can gain astonishing insights by interpreting a genogram, a graphic representation of the personalities and interplay of generations within a family. Most individuals would be amazed by the amount of information conveyed by this psychological family tree. A genogram can reveal fertile grounds for exploration of family systems issues, including strengths and dysfunctions. Many patterns of behavior recur frequently within the family system over generations.

193. What is said in a conversation is not nearly as important as what is heard.

Communication involves a dual relationship running in one or both directions between a speaker and a listener. What a speaker intends to convey may easily be misunderstood by the

192. A detailed graph of the psychological family tree reveals the motivations of individual family members.

listener because of different contexts or frames of reference. Anger, stress, confusion, or even soft voices in a noisy room can inhibit concise and accurate communications.

Overuse of pronouns and vague references are also threats. The speaker has a burden of making sure that the listener receives the message accurately. Similarly, the listener needs to confirm the message from the speaker. Surely, many wars have started because of poor communications.

194. Angry words and hurt, unresolved and unforgiven, threaten the golden goose.

195. Angry words sound louder in a large home.

Wealthy siblings or spouses have numerous weapons to wage a loud war of words. Rich folks can allocate resources to long-term shouting contests, lawsuits, separation, divorce, or a test of wills between parents and children.

Arguments extract a high cost in terms of valuable resources; eventually, continual emotional battles translate into depression.

Loud arguments then evolve into long silences, which also are amplified in a large home.

196. In stressful situations, conversation that should take place between two family members will be carried out through triangulation with a third person.

Avoid such triangles, which can become spider webs in the family.

---

197. It is okay to have strong differences of opinion in the family—that means there is open communication. Ending arguments in a healthy manner is the hard part.

---

198. Owning one-fifth of five thousand acres of land with family members is more impressive than owning one thousand acres on your own.

People are much more impressed if you can say "we own five thousand acres over in X County" than it is to say "we own a thousand acres in X County."

Sole ownership of a parcel of real estate (or a business interest) may have more power associated with it, but shared ownership may carry more clout and offer more personal satisfaction. In many cases, co-ownership among siblings and their respective families is undertaken out of respect for the family members who established the legacy. Sometimes, co-ownership is imposed through wills and trusts.

Enjoy the clout and notoriety that goes along with owning a small piece of a bigger pie. If storm clouds gather, it is usually easy to partition the property and let each family unit rule a smaller kingdom.

199. In a purchase and sale between family members, true fair market value is not nearly as important as the process of reaching agreement.

Even the best appraisers can't pinpoint the exact fair market value of a substantial asset— a farm, apartment building, or a closely held business—shared by a number of family members. Only cash and marketable securities are free from substantial dispute.

The reason is that each family member owns a small piece of the larger asset. The value of all of the small pieces do not, together, equal the fair market value of the whole asset. This may seem to defy explanation, but the value of a ten percent interest by itself in a large family-owned business is much less than ten percent of the proceeds received from a sale of the entire family business.

Fair market value for an undivided interest in a large indivisible asset varies widely. In a sale within the family, all members should avoid shopping for a favorable appraisal. The appropriate value should (more or less) reflect what the family or company can afford to pay and, at the same time, how much the selling family should expect to receive.

Glenn Ayres, in an article in *Family Business Review* called "Rough Family Justice: Equity in the Family Business Succession Planning" (Vol. II, No. 1, Spring 1990, pp. 3-22), clearly explains factors that are more appropriate for reaching family consensus than commissioning several disparate appraisals. The standard should be a fair price, not fair market value.

200. In wealthy families, women place importance on the family, but men place importance on the family business or wealth.

This is a broad generality, but women are usually more connected with the emotion-based family system, whereas men connect to the technical-based business system. Recognize that a mother and father may have different priorities for establishing and pursuing specific goals. Try to have a healthy balance between family-based priorities and business and financial priorities.

THE REAL WORLD

Dan and Jane are in their mid-sixties. Their two children, ages forty and forty-two, are happily married with children of their own. Dan owns a very successful automobile dealership. His son works in the business, but his daughter does not.

Dan really didn't need professional help with his estate plan or his succession plan. He had already figured it out: fifty-one percent to his son and forty-nine percent to his daughter.

Epilogue: Dan thinks his son loves his sister and would treat her and her family fairly. Everyone but Dad has doubts about the son's ability to run the dealership. Jane senses the pending disaster, but she has been unsuccessful in getting her family to sit down and talk about these matters together.

Dan hates spending money on lawyers, accountants, and consultants. He doesn't want anyone "planning his life for him." He thinks nothing bad is going to happen as long as he is alive and healthy.

The family will never be able to communicate because telling the truth is going to frustrate and disappoint Dan. Jane hopes only that she will be able to "balance things" after Dan's death.

I predict that not long after Dan's death, the family will sell the dealership.

Professionally Speaking...

Consultants experienced with wealthy family groups and family-owned businesses know that their job is not to analyze information and create a comprehensive financial and estate plan for the family. Such documents designed to carry out a complex plan often collect dust because the family makes one excuse or another for postponing final decision-making.

The consultant should facilitate a communication process between family members as they explore options, discuss pros and cons, and together reach important decisions for developing and implementing a final plan.

They need multidisciplinary and holistic talents, in addition to technical skills and proficiency, to accomplish the task. It is not a question of whether business issues are more important than family issues. It is a matter of engaging in a healthy process of communication that finds balance between the two.

Related axioms from Chapter 1

1. Mom is the most powerful member of the family.

2. The wife is CEO—Chief Emotional Officer—of the family.

3. Financial planning for the family is pointless until absolute financial security is assured for Mom.

7. Accept the responsibility to learn about raising wealthy children—do not try to make it up as you go.

8. Many rich fathers deny that family emotional issues need psychological tools. They try to deal with every issue in terms of power, money, or control.

10. Increased longevity can be a financial disaster for children of well-to-do parents.

11. Be thoughtful when the kids ask, "Are we rich?"

12. If being rich is good, why do rich parents keep it a secret from the kids—really?

13. Rich kids resent not being trusted with family wealth secrets.

14. Don't use wealth to control family members from the grave.

15. Rich parents should not try to use wealth to control, direct, or influence decisions that children need to make for themselves.

16. Each child is different—take care to customize your approach to teaching and raising each one.

19. Your wife tells you how wonderful and right you are, regardless of the objective truth—that's why you married her in the first place.

Related axioms from Chapter 2

24. Rich families should not act embarrassed about disabled children.

29. It may not be best for the children, and future generations of the family, to share ownership of assets.

26. Use trust funds to support children who work for other reasons than money.

27. Don't push a round peg into a square hole. Help each child find his or her slot in life, even if it's not what you want.

28. Maybe Junior doesn't want to run the family business. Can he tell you this without hurting you?

32. Rich fathers will struggle to balance financial benefits for two sets of children if they don't communicate with everybody.

39. It is impossible to treat all children equally, so stop trying.

40. Is equal really fair?

50. Money can't buy perfect children.

51. Teaching children does not include controlling their lives or protecting them from the consequences of their bad decisions.

52. In measuring your children's ability to be responsible and accountable, take note of their listening skills.

54. To the Next Generation: "Are you ready, today, to accept responsibility for assets and wealth?"

57. In a new-wealth family, older children are often more appreciative of having money.

Related axioms from Chapter 3

63. Rich widow to friend: "I'd like to pull him out of the grave and shoot him."
   —Joy Culverhouse, *The Tampa Tribune,* 2/2/97.

68. If children don't share equal responsibility for caring for their parents, the family must have a clear understanding about financial expectations.

71. Why is it a fourteen-year-old can't drive a car, get married, or control substantial assets, but his ninety-year-old grandparent can?

72. Why won't the old man let go of control—really?

74. The greatest loss of wealth occurs when the person controlling it fails to identify his or her own senility, dementia, or other mental impairment.

Related axioms from Chapter 4

84. In some cases, a dying spouse may need to ask the survivor to protect their children by a prenuptial agreement with a future spouse.

Related axioms from Chapter 5

88. Rich parents are reluctant to transfer wealth to their children for fear much will be lost in a divorce.

91. Before you name your brother as trustee, remember he is busy with his own life and family needs.

105. Before you name your brother as executor, consider items 91–95 above.

106. Before you name your oldest child as executor, remember he or she never did get along with brothers and sisters growing up.

Related axioms from Chapter 6

109. Be suspicious if your daughter-in-law admires your jewelry, art, silver, china, and crystal.

110. Be suspicious if your son-in-law admires your boat and vacation home.

113. Woe be unto the daughter-in-law who takes sides in a family dispute.

115. Two spouses in a second marriage create a disaster for the family of the first spouse to die by trying to share a simple estate plan.

Related axioms from Chapter 7

117. Pass the torch, but be sure to tell the recipient it's hot.

118. Passing the torch doesn't have to mean burning down the family tree.

123. It is better to accept the fact that issues are interrelated in a circle than to struggle down a spiral staircase.

124. The process of direct, honest, and regular communications within the family is the key to future successorship and legacy.

126. Conduct an emergency fire drill; what will happen if you die or become incapacitated today?

127. Consider dictating your hopes, beliefs, wishes, thoughts, and suggestions for the family and the business after your death or incapacity.

128. The time, effort, and expense of strategic family business planning greatly increases the odds of success.

129. Be suspicious when a family member insists that he or she must have fifty-one percent of the voting power.

131. Don't assume that cousins will always vote along family branches.

132. Why do people with power, money, and control try to make decisions without knowing all the facts, alternatives, and lessons from others?

133. The golden goose that produces bounty for only one master will be divided into many parts at the master's death.

134. You can face your own mortality if you can voluntarily surrender power, money, and control to your successors.

137. Family history, culture, and values greatly impact family business ownership and management.

Related axiom from Chapter 9

154. Many family businesses will be sold for a lot of money some day; the beneficiaries often lack experience with financial and investment planning.

Related axioms from Chapter 10

161. Family limited partnerships are good estate planning devices, but they may not be good for your family.

164. Negative thoughts lead to shutdown in the planning process.

166. Discussion is difficult because many issues overlap and are interdependent.

Related axioms from Chapter 12

177. The satisfaction and joy of building wealth is much different from the satisfaction and joy of inheriting it.

178. A sudden change from non-wealth to wealth will disrupt some family relationships. Be prepared, be sensitive, and be patient.

Related axiom from Chapter 14

189. Families that work together need lives of their own.

Annotated Bibliography

Chapter 1

Danco, Katy. *From the Other Side of the Bed: A Woman Looks at Life in the Family Business.* Cleveland: The Center for Family Business-University Press, 1981.

• I made a serious mistake in failing to read this book in earlier years; I incorrectly presumed this was a work by the incomparable Leon Danco's wife written merely to relieve boredom. The book includes outstanding chapters and case studies that clarify the challenges and issues for women in a family business setting; the discussion concerning in-laws is particularly good. This is an excellent book to share with clients.

Davis, John A. and Renato Tagiuri. "The Influence of Life Stage on Father-Son Work Relationships in Family Companies." *Family Business Review* 2, no. 1 (Spring 1989): 47-74.

Chapter 2

Barber, Judy G. "Transferring Assets: Is It Good for Your Children?" *Family Money,* Fall 1995.

Barnes, Louis B. "Incongruent Hierarchies: Daughters and Younger Sons as Company CEO's." *Family Business Review* 1, no. 1 (Spring 1988): 9-21.

_____. "Daughters Find that Fathers Still Resist Passing the Family Business on to Them." *The Wall Street Journal,* 14 April 1992.

Editor. "To a son, on his entering the business." *Family Business,* May 1990, 42-45.

Frankenberg, "Ellen. "Raising Your Daughter to be the Next CEO." *Family Business*, Summer 1996, 45-49.

Godfrey, Neale S. and Carolina Edwards. *Money Doesn't Grow on Trees: A Parent's Guide to Raising Financially Responsible Children.* New York: Fireside, 1994.

• This very basic guide helps parents educate young children, adolescents, and teenagers about money and finances. The book contains common-sense tips, exercises, and suggestions for a training process that is often neglected—especially in wealthy families who have the most at risk.

Grady, Katherine. "Is the family business right for me?" *Family Business,* Spring 2000, 55-61.

_____. "Growing Up Wealthy and Healthy: Raising Rich Kids." *Transforming Business Families:* 79-84.

Pearl, Jayne A. *Kids and Money.* Princeton, N.J.: Bloomberg Press, 1999.

• Wealthy family members are increasingly aware of the need to prepare children for their future roles in the utilization, stewardship, preservation, and responsibilities of wealth. This book is not deep on substance and analysis, but it provides helpful stimulation in beginning to address these important issues.

Pearl-Hommell, Jayne. "Getting off the daughter track." *Family Business,* March, 1990, 28-31.

_____. "Too young to drive, old enough for college." *Forbes*, 12 June 2000.

Chapter 3

Hobbs, Steven H. and Fay Wilson Hobbs. "The Ethical Management of Assets for Elder Clients: A Context, Role, and Law Approach." *Fordham Law Review* 62, no. 5 (March 1994): 1411-1428.

Chapter 4

Baker, Debra. "Wealthy Wives' Tales." *ABA Journal*, July 1998, 72-76.

Barber, Judy. "Surviving Prenuptial Agreements." *Family Money,* Winter 1995, 1-3.

Belcher, Dennis I. and Laura O. Pomeroy. "For Richer, for Poorer: Strategies for Premarital Agreements." *Probate & Property,* November/December 1998, 55-59.

Flanagan, William G. and David Stix. "Share and share unalike." *Forbes*, 10 June 1991, 116-120.

Fraser, Jill Andresky. "Divorce-proofing your company." *Inc.,* September 1998, 92-101.

Freedman, Michael. "For Love and Money." *Forbes,* 11 June 2001.

McMenamin, Brigid. "'Til divorce do us part." *Forbes,* 14 October 14 1996.

Mendoza, Drew S. and Sharon P. Krone. "An Interview with Judy G. Barber: Prenuptial Agreement, Intimacy, Trust and Control." *Family Business Review* 10, no. 1 (Spring 1997): 173-184.

Schoenberger, Chana. "'Til Lawyers Do Us Part." *Forbes,* 27 December 1999.

Chapter 5

Geer, Carolyn T. "Trust a trust." *Forbes,* 14 August 1995.

Jones, Bernard E. "Putting Revocable Trusts in Their Place." *Trusts & Estates,* September 1990, 8-19.

Kemp, George. "Acceptance of Accounts with a Closely-Held Business Interest." *Trusts & Estates,* June 1992, 46-48.

Lehman, Mary B. "Managing a Business Interest in Trust." *Family Business Review* 5, no. 2 (Summer 1992): 137-143.

Levy, John L. "Prisoners of distrust." *Family Business*, Winter 1997, 49-51.

Nager, Ross W. "The Trustee of Your Dreams." *Family Business,* Summer 1994, 47-51.

Chapter 6

Jonovic, Donald J. "Ignore Your In-Laws." *Family Inc.,* Summer 1997, 8-10.

LeVan, Gerald. "Daughters-In-Law: Navigating in Troubled Waters." *Family Business,* April 1990, 66-67.

Papernow, Patricia L. *Becoming a Stepfamily.* San Francisco: Jossey-Bass, 1993.
• This book is an insightful discussion about the patterns of development in remarried families, an increasingly common issue with special implications for family-owned businesses and various family units. Sensitive questions about participation in the family legacy by stepchildren are well worth exploring, and this book is very informative on the subject.

Chapter 7

Aronoff, Craig E. and others. Family Business Leadership Series. Marietta, Georgia: Family Enterprise Publishers, 1995.

• This landmark series make difficult topics easy to read and understand. Although the material is from the "soft" side, the booklets present a fair amount of technical information to analyze issues and possible solutions. Makes a great gift for clients or family members.

Ayres, Glenn R. *Rough Corporate Justice.* Fredrickson & Byron, The Family Business Alliance.

Ayres, Glenn R. "Rough Family Justice: Equity in the Family Business Succession Planning." *Family Business Review* 2, no. 1 (Spring 1990): 3-22.

Barach, Jeffrey A. "Successful Succession in Family Business." *Family Business Review* 8, no. 2 (1992): 131-155.

Danco, Léon and Donald J. Jonovic. *Someday It'll All Be ... Who's?—The Lighter Side of the Family Business.* Cleveland: The Center for Family Business, 1990.
• This entertaining collection of family business cartoons evoke serious issues that face family business owners and other family members. This a great book to pass around the family, but be forewarned that some of the jokes will hit close to home.

Editors, *Family Business* magazine. *The Family Business Succession Handbook.* Philadelphia: Family Business Publishing Company, Inc., 1997.

- *Family Business* magazine has compiled its best case studies, interviews, and articles on dealing with the issue of family business successorship and the transfer of leadership and ownership to the next generation.

Family Business magazine. Philadelphia: Family Business Publishing Company, Inc.

- This quarterly magazine is an excellent way to keep family business themes at the forefront; articles address the specific and unique needs and demands of the family business. With a very easy-to-read writing style, it is the only resource of this nature.

Gersick, Kelin E. "The Cousins Tournament." *Family Business,* Winter 1995, 30-39.

Hubler, Thomas J. "Ten Most Prevalent Obstacles to Family-Business Succession Planning." *Family Business Review* 12, no. 2 (June 1999): 117-121.

Jaffe, Dennis T. *Working With the Ones You Love—Strategies for a Successful Family Business.* Berkeley, Cal.: Conari Press, 1990.

- The author explores the key concepts in successorship planning in a workbook and discussion format. This book is used in college courses that deal with family business matters and is an excellent resource for training. It addresses more of the psychological side of issues—a very readable introduction into the "soft" issues that must be understood and addressed.

Lansberg, Ivan. The Succession Conspiracy. *Family Business Review* 1, no. 2 (September 1988): 119-143.

Lansberg, Ivan. "Twelve Tasks in Succession." *Family Business,* Summer 1993, 18-24.

Shapiro, Harvey D. "When Family Shareholders Want Out." *Family Business,* March/April 1991, 27-30.

Chapter 8

Collier, Charles W. *Wealth in Families.* Cambridge, Mass.: Harvard University Press, 2001.

- This is an articulate and well-written book by an academician very familiar with the needs, habits, and patterns of wealthy families. He pulls no punches—he wants to persuade wealthy families to take careful measure of the amounts they leave to children and grandchildren, while giving more attention to stewardship and philanthropy. He recognizes that wealthy individuals have a significant opportunity to make a difference in the community they should not miss.

Comstock, Paul L. "Financial Parenting Through a Family Foundation." *Trusts & Estates,* August 1992, 32-38.

Ebeling, Ashlea. "Keeping Up With the Gateses." *Forbes,* 11 December 2000, 274-276.

Frankenberg, Ellen. *"Beyond enough: The joy-to-stuff ratio."* Family Business, Summer 1999, 59-64.

Karoff, H. Peter. "The Advisor's Role in Philanthropy: A New Direction." *Trusts & Estates,* April 1994.

Newman, David W. and Jose Silva. "A Look at Alternatives to Private Foundations." *Trusts & Estates,* August 1994, 10-19, 61.

Stone, Deanne. Glue to Bind Generations. *Family Business,* Summer 1994, 41-46.

Chapter 10

Capassakis, Evelyn M. "Top 10 Estate Planning Strategies (Part I)." *The Tax Advisor,* January 2001, 26-37.

Capassakis, Evelyn M. "Top 10 Estate Planning Strategies (Part II)." *The Tax Advisor,* February 2001, 110-116.

Coplan, Roger B., et al. "Succession Planning for Wealthy Family Groups." *Trusts & Estates,* November 1994, 31-39.

Drew, Christopher and David Cay Johnston. "For Wealthy Americans, Death is More Certain than Taxes." *The New York Times,* 22 December 1996.

Hopkins, John F. "Equality is often unfair." *Family Business,* Summer 1997, 45-50.

Prestopino, Chris J. "Strategies Recommended by Experienced Estate Planner." *Trusts & Estates,* January 1994, 47-54.

Schiller, Keith. "Prozac® and Estate Planning for Families." *Trusts & Estates,* November 1998, 73-77.

Chapter 11

Aronoff, Craig E. and John L. Ward. *How to Choose and Use Advisors: Getting the Best Professional Family Business Advice.* Family Business Leadership Series. Marietta, Ga.: Family Enterprise Publishers, 1994.

Ricker, Di Mari. "My Lawyer Sent Me Flowers." *ABA Journal,* April 1996, 78-82.

Swartz, Stephen. "The Challenges of Multidisciplinary Consulting to Family-Owned Businesses." *Family Business Review* 2, no. 4 (Winter 1989): 329-339.

Upton, Nancy, et al. "Research Note: Family Business Consultants—Who We Are, What We Do, and How We Do It." *Family Business Review* 6, no. 3 (Fall 1993): 301-311.

Zebel, William D. "Time Out for the Human Side of Estate Planning." *Trusts & Estates,* May 1988, 8-20.

Chapter 12

Blouin, Barbara with Katherine Gibson and Margaret Kiersted. *The Legacy of Inherited Wealth: Interviews with Heirs*. Blacksburg, Va.: The Inheritance Project, 1995.

- This collection of stories and interviews reveals the windfalls, struggles, and challenges faced by several individuals who inherited wealth. Sadly, they have little joy and satisfaction to discuss. The book is especially helpful for suddenly wealthy individuals seeking confirmation, understanding, and a sense of empathy.

Domini, Amy L. with Dennis Pearne and Sharon L. Rich. *The Challenges of Wealth—Mastering the Personal and Financial Conflicts*. Homewood, Ill.: Dow Jones-Irwin, 1988.

- This interesting analysis of the nature of wealth is not limited to closely held family business interests. In fact, it is more applicable to liquid wealth in the form of cash, marketable securities, and real estate that generates substantial income. The authors deal with the emotional and financial challenges of wealth, addressing the needs, concerns, interests, and viewpoints of various family members confronted with the pleasant, but serious, challenges of being wealthy. I like this one for its unique perspective on a difficult topic.

Rogal, Keith H. "Obligation or Opportunity: How Can Could-Be Heirs Assess Their Position?" *Family Business Review* 2, no. 3 (Fall 1989): 237-255.

Rottenberg, Dan. *The Inheritor's Handbook*. Princeton, N.J.: Bloomberg Press, 1999.

- This guide includes advice on managing an inheritance successfully, retaining professional services, and other issues. Using first-hand experiences, the author deals with both financial and emotional issues faced by beneficiaries of inherited wealth. I like the book because it is well-organized and easy to read. Complex trust and tax issues are discussed in common English rather than technical language.

Chapter 13

Benson, Benjamin, et al. "Calling the family to order." *Family Business,* February 1990, 34-35.

Doud, Ernest A., Jr. and Lee Hausner. "Family Meetings and Family Retreats." Excerpt from *Hats Off to You: Balancing Roles and Creating Success in Family Business*. Glendale, Cal.: Doud/Hausner & Associates, 2000.

Family Office Exchange, Madison, N.J., foxexchange.com.

Grace, Charles. "The Multiple Client Family Office." *Trusts & Estates,* February 2000, 54-55.

Henning, Mike. "Who's afraid of a family council?" *Family Business,* Autumn 1998, 48-54.

Lansberg, Ivan. "The best investment a family will ever make." *Family Business,* Winter 1997, 9-10, 71.

Lasky, Jane E. "When the Best Course is Retreat." *Family Business,* March 1990, 64-69.

Lenzner, Robert and Scott McCormack. "Achieving immortality via the family office." *Forbes 400,* 12 October 1998, 47-58.

Chapter 14

Aronoff, Craig E. and John L. Ward. *Family Business Values: How to Assure a Legacy of Continuity and Success.* Family Business Leadership Series. Marietta, Ga.: Family Enterprise Publishers, 2000.

Lansberg, Ivan. "Succeeding Generations: Realizing the Dream of Families in Business." *Family Business Review* 12, no. 2 (June 1999): 189-192.

Chapter 15

Cole, Patricia M. "Women in Family Business." *Family Business Review* 10, no. 4 (December 1997): 353-371.

Dashew, Leslie. *The Best of the Human Side.* Atlanta, Ga.: Human Side of Enterprise, 1997.

• Written by a respected organizational development consultant and family therapist, this collection of articles is excellent book for attorneys, accountants, and other technical-based professionals who need a better understanding of the touchy-feely side of family business issues. Probably a little heavy for family members.

Frankenberg, Ellen. *Your Family, Inc.* Binghampton, N.Y.: Haworth Press, 1999.

• The author is a well-known family psychologist who specializes in consulting with families in business together. This book definitely represents the soft side of multi-disciplinary practice. It is a good choice for a first book to share with clients and families who are just beginning to work on problems associated with successorship. Its more holistic approach will be more comfortable to family members not directly active in the family business.

Friedman, Michael and Scott Friedman. *How to Run a Family Business.* Cincinnati, Ohio: F&W Publications, 1994.

• This book takes a broad look at the many legal issues that confront families owning a business enterprise together. Light reading, it deals with relatively basic topics—structure of the business, compensation, financing the business, shareholder agreements, and other basic matters. The book offers helpful technical information, but it fails to penetrate the issues involved with family dynamics and systems in relation to business dynamics and systems.

Harvey, Michael, et al. "Family Business and Multiple Levels of Conflict." *Family Business Review* 7, no. 4 (Winter 1994): 331-348.

Hilbert-Davis, Jane and W. Gibb Dyer. *Consulting to Family Businesses.* Hoboken, N.J.: Jossey-Bass/Wiley, 2003.

• The authors update and advance the role of the family business consultant. This is the modern definition of the holistic, qualified, and effective consultant. An excellent resource for families and advisors.

ANNOTATED BIBLIOGRAPHY

Hughes, James E. *Family Wealth: Keeping It In the Family.* Princeton, N.J.: NetWrx, 1997.

- Jay Hughes is a trusted advisor and counselor for several wealthy family groups. He emphasizes the personal and emotional factors should be considered in the preservation of family wealth. Almost half of the book is a chapter entitled "My Philosophy on Long-Term Preservation of Family Wealth, Theory and Practice." Jay has the credentials and experience to give advice of this nature.

Koenig, Neil N. *You Can't Fire Me—I'm Your Father! (What Every Family Business Should Know).* Franklin, Tenn.: Hillsboro Press, 1999.

- This book clearly reflects the author's background as clergy, family psychologist, and management consultant. Its rambling structure is loose and informal. It does an excellent job of analyzing specific family issues such as grief, Alzheimer's, and getting along as a family. A good book for family business advisors needing additional information about the family side of issues.

Lansberg, Ivan. *Succeeding Generations.* Boston: Harvard Business School Press, 1999.

- This is unequivocally one of the best books I have ever read about dealing with families who own a business enterprise together. The author is well-experienced in the family business consulting community. He is one of the best—and this book shows why. The latter chapters dealing with governance structures and processes for continuity are bold and refreshing. He offers specific advice and new thinking on critically important topics. I believe the author presents some of the most important developments since the early work of Danco and Ward. The information is a little heavy; it requires patience and a fairly strong background and understanding of family and business dynamics to appreciate some of the author's concepts and theories.

Lea, James W. *Keeping it in the Family—Successful Succession of the Family Business.* New York: John Wiley & Sons, 1991.

- This book analyzes the unique nature of a family business, explains why a successorship plan is necessary, and sets out specific guidelines to follow in taking a family business to the next generation. Easy to read.

LeVan, Gerald. *The $urvival Guide for Business Families.* New York: Routledge Press, 1999.

- This is one of my favorite books for family business owners. The author is a true leader in the field with many years of direct experience. He has developed the principal case study in the book—JacMar Corporation—over the past eight to ten years into the most thorough and comprehensive family business example in the area. Warning: The author occasionally expresses strong opinions that are not necessarily true in all cases.

Liebman, Betsy G. "Breaking shareholder deadlocks." *Family Business,* Winter 1999, 59-62.

Syms, Marcy. *Mind Your Own Business—Keep it in the Family.* New York: MasterMedia Limited, 1992.

Tagiuri, Renato and John Davis. "Bivalent Attributes of the Family Firm." *Family Business Review* 9, no. 2 (Summer 1996): 199-208.

Ward, John F. *Keeping the Family Business Healthy.* Marietta, Ga.: Family Enterprise Publishers, 1987.

• One of the standards in the field, this book encourages families to undertake the process of successorship. It contains details and materials concerning development of a strategic business plan. An older book, but not out of date.

Whiteside, Mary F. *How Families Work Together.* Family Business Leadership Series. Marietta, Ga.: Family Enterprise Publishers, 1987.

Withrow, Scott C. "Integrating Family Business Systems in Succession Planning." *The Practical Lawyer,* April 1997, 81-92.

Appendix A

DECLARATION

We are fortunate and grateful to be the children of _____. We consider ourselves lucky to be a part of a very loving and caring family. It is difficult to think about the prospect of leaving the nest to start a family of our own. The memory and experiences, and the continuation of our special family relationships, prepare us well for our next steps in life.

It seems we never thought about money while we were kids. We appreciate now how lucky we have been to have everything we really ever needed, and a whole lot more. We have begun to figure out that we are a privileged family from the standpoint of money and financial resources. We are embarrassed to admit it, but I guess we are wealthy when compared to almost every other family. Thank you for sharing some of this information with us so we can better understand it. Thank you for the gifts and trusts that you have already given us. We sometimes feel embarrassed because we do not deserve it. You built it and you earned it.

We encourage you to keep everything that you need for a very happy and comfortable life together for as long as God allows. If there is anything left, we will be grateful to receive it and use it for the betterment of ourselves and our own families. We have received much from both of you already in terms of money, stock, and trust accounts. We may receive a lot more in future years. Thank you for trusting us with these assets before you die.

We have made a promise to ourselves after talking about it. We want to make a declaration to you and to each other that we promise to be good stewards of any wealth that happens to come our way from you now or later. We feel a deep sense of duty and obligation concerning these assets. We hereby declare our acceptance of the responsibilities which go with these gifts.

First of all, we look forward to the opportunity to choose our partners in marriage. And, if God is willing, to raise families of our own. We hope our marriage can be like yours. We expect to embrace, love, and cherish our marriage partner. This will include trust, devotion, and fidelity. We will want to share everything with them. At the same time, we are mindful of the need to separate our family wealth from the assets that we are able to accumulate with our individual marriage partners. We will use our gifted or inherited family resources for the betterment of our families and to give us opportunities that may be otherwise unobtainable. At the same time, we promise to keep our family wealth separated through all possible steps that are appropriate and legal. The bottom line is that we know about prenuptial agreements and what they mean. We have talked about it and thought about it. All of us promise to enter into such agreements with our marriage partners. We are confident that our future partners will understand and respect this decision. We owe this to you, our siblings, and ourselves.

Also, and equally important, we declare our intentions to be exceptionally good stewards of our wealth. We will always adequately provide for our family. But we also accept the responsibility to use wealth for the benefit of those who are less fortunate than ourselves. We will support our religious institutions, our educational institutions, and other charitable organizations devoted to the health and welfare of less fortunate people. We see what you have done, and what you are doing, and we are committed to continuing this work in honor of both of you. Thank you for giving us the opportunity to deal with these duties and responsibilities. Thank you for everything.